Web
geek's
Guide

to the

Android™-Enabled Phone

Jerri Ledford
Bill Zimmerly
Prasanna Amirthalingam

800 East 96th Street,
Indianapolis, Indiana 46240

Web Geek's Guide to the Android™-Enabled Phone

ISBN-13: 978-0-7897-3972-8
ISBN-10: 0-7897-3972-0

Library of Congress Cataloging-in-Publication Data:

Ledford, Jerri L.

Web geek's guide to the Android-enabled phone / Jerri Ledford, Bill Zimmerly, Prasanna Amirthalingam.— 1st ed.

    p. cm.

  ISBN 978-0-7897-3972-8

1. G1 (Smartphone) 2. Android (Electronic resource) 3. Cellular telephones. 4. Google. I. Zimmerly, Bill. II. Amirthalingam, Prasanna. III. Title. IV. Title: Android-enabled phone.

  TK6570.M6L32 2010

  621.3845'6—dc22

                            2009032560

Printed in the United States of America

First Printing: September 2009

Trademarks

Warning and Disclaimer

Bulk Sales

Que Publishing offers excellent discounts on this book when ordered in quantity for bulk purchases or special sales. For more information, please contact

    U.S. Corporate and Government Sales
    1-800-382-3419
    corpsales@pearsontechgroup.com

For sales outside of the U.S., please contact

    International Sales
    international@pearson.com

Associate Publisher
Greg Wiegand

Acquisitions Editor
Michelle Newcomb

Development Editor
Todd Brakke

Managing Editor
Kristy Hart

Project Editor
Andy Beaster

Copy Editor
Krista Hansing Editorial Services

Indexer
WordWise Publishing Solutions LLC

Proofreader
Debbie Williams

Technical Editor
Brice Mason

Publishing Coordinator
Cindy Teeters

Cover Designer
Ann Jones

Compositor
Nonie Ratcliff

Contents at a Glance

Table of Contents

Appendixes

About the Authors

Jerri Ledford has been a freelance business technology writer for more than 10 years. During that time, more than 1,000 of her articles, profiles, news stories, and reports have appeared online and in print. Her publishing credits include *Intelligent Enterprise, Network World, Information Security Magazine, DCM Magazine, CRM Magazine, IT Manager's Journal,* and dozens more.

Jerri also develops and teaches technology training courses for both consumer and business users. Some of the course topics she's been involved with include security, customer service, career skills, and technology for companies such as IBT Financial, Writer's Village University, Beacon Hill Financial Services, Hewlett-Packard, Sony, and CNET.

She is the author of 17 books, including these:

- *The Web Geek's Guide to Google Chrome*
- *Google Powered: Productivity with Online Tools*
- *Google Analytics 2.0*

In her free time, Jerri travels extensively and enjoys hiking, writing fiction novels, and soaking up the positive ions at the beach with her children.

Bill Zimmerly is a retired computer programmer with interests that include writing about and programming Linux-powered gadgets like Android cell phones and Web applications for the Internet. With "tongue in cheek" sarcasm Bill considers himself one of those "unreasonable" men that the great writer Mr. George Bernard Shaw wrote about when he penned the famous line, "The reasonable man adapts himself to the world. The unreasonable man persists in trying to adapt the world to himself. All progress, therefore, depends upon the unreasonable man."

Prasanna Amirthalingam is a software engineer who develops applications on both Java and .NET. He is very passionate about developing applications and loves sharing his passion through technical speaking and technical writing.

He has authored exam content for more than 15 certification exams on various Microsoft technologies, including .NET, VSTS, VSTO, and Mobile development, and has been a Microsoft MVP since 2005. He loves travelling and has been working in different countries after starting his technical career in the beautiful islands of Sri Lanka. You can read his blog at www.prasanna.ws.

Dedication

From Jerri Ledford:

For my children, because of all the people in the world, you always believe in me. Thanks, guys. I love you. —Mom

Acknowledgments

Jerri Ledford

It takes so many people to put a book together. And not all of them end up on the cover.

Lynn Haller is one of those whose name has been on covers, just not this one. It deserves to be on every one, though. Without Lynn, the book would never have found a home. It takes considerable work on Lynn's part every time I get a wild hair and decide to write a book. I'm eternally grateful to her for that.

Michelle Newcomb and the team at Que are also to be commended. I don't know all of their names, or even fully understand what they all do, but I'm so very thankful for all of their efforts. My part in this book was easy; it's the people behind the scenes who really make a book successful.

Finally, thanks to the readers, as always, for picking up this book. I hope you find everything you're looking for in these pages.

Bill Zimmerly

I would like to offer a very special thank you to Jerri Ledford, for inviting me to participate in its creation. I want to thank the people of Studio B Productions—especially Lynn Haller and Renee Midrack—without whom I would not have been a contributor to this project. To Michelle Newcomb of Pearson Publishing for presenting me with this opportunity and to the various editors who assisted us in the project—Todd Brakke, Brice Mason, Krista Hansing, Prasanna, among others.

I would like to thank my family for their love and support not only during this project, but also for all of my life. People born to loving families such as mine are indeed very fortunate and I am grateful for them all.

Finally, I dedicate this book to three very special friends who have meant the world to me since I have known them—(1) my best friend since High School—Rick Nolle, (2) a close friend and great radio personality—Lloyd Sloan (aka "The Sloan Ranger"), and (3) my Amateur Radio mentor and friend, Tom Vogel, call sign WA0KGU. May God bless you all my friends, family, and colleagues!

We Want to Hear from You!

As the reader of this book, *you* are our most important critic and commentator. We value your opinion and want to know what we're doing right, what we could do better, what areas you'd like to see us publish in, and any other words of wisdom you're willing to pass our way.

As an associate publisher for Que Publishing, I welcome your comments. You can email or write me directly to let me know what you did or didn't like about this book—as well as what we can do to make our books better.

Please note that I cannot help you with technical problems related to the topic of this book. We do have a User Services group, however, where I will forward specific technical questions related to the book.

When you write, please be sure to include this book's title and author as well as your name, email address, and phone number. I will carefully review your comments and share them with the author and editors who worked on the book.

Email: feedback@quepublishing.com

Mail: Greg Wiegand
Associate Publisher
Que Publishing
800 East 96th Street
Indianapolis, IN 46240 USA

Reader Services

Visit our website and register this book at www.informit.com/title/ 9780789739728 for convenient access to any updates, downloads, or errata that might be available for this book.

Introduction

We live in a time when everything in our lives has to do double duty. Cars serve not only as cars but also as traveling offices, and dinner dates become business meetings or event-planning sessions. So it's no surprise that our devices must also do more than just be a phone, an MP3 player, or a GPS unit. If a device can be all of those, so much the better.

Then there's the Web. We use the Web for everything these days. We don't look up phone numbers anymore; we Google them. We don't look up movies; we Google them. And we don't use a dictionary, thesaurus, map, or cookbook anymore; we Google all the information we need.

In fact, Google is the most used search engine today. And upon activating a web-enabled device, one of the first things people do is open a web browser and navigate to Google.

Google isn't blind to this fact. In fact, the company monitors the number of mobile devices that access the Google search engine and other Google applications. Combine that information with the data that's available about the number of web-enabled mobile devices sold each year—about a billion—and then mix in user behavior. Clearly, we need a web-based operating system that is designed to work well on a mobile platform, enabled with all manner of applications to meet user demands.

The Birth of Android

Enter Andy Rubin and his Android idea. Rubin approached Google seeking financing for his idea. He got a purchase offer that lit the rumor mills on fire. Suddenly, the buzz on the Net was that Google would soon release a cellphone to compete with other web-enabled cellphones.

That wasn't quite true. Google wants no part in manufacturing mobile phones and devices. Manufacturing isn't the company's core competency, and branching into devices would take away precious resources from what Google does best: web-based applications.

Instead, the company spearheaded the Open Handset Alliance. Working with more than 40 companies in the alliance, Google developed the core for a new mobile operating system: Android. But Android is more than just an operating system; it enables developers to create web-based applications that work together with the device to give users truly useful programs.

Now stir into the mix a healthy dose of open source programming, and you've got a whole new way to think about mobile development. In the past, Apple has been the most successful company to develop mobile applications. But Apple keeps a tight rein on developers. Applications must be approved before they're released, and the company isn't keen on allowing multiple apps at the same time in the Apple Marketplace.

What's more, Apple's process of approving an application is long and arduous. Some developers who have created applications specifically for the iPhone or iPod waited weeks before Apple ultimately turned them down.

Android is truly different. Because it's open source, people can use it to collaboratively develop applications. Developers can build applications that become the basis for new applications. All applications have access to the core applications and hardware of an Android-based device.

The Android Market also has the true spirit of open source. Developers are welcome to create applications that they think will be useful and can upload them to the Android Market for other users to access for free or through purchase. Developers simply pay a $25 registration fee and agree to adhere to a simple set of guidelines, basically stating that the developers will do their best to produce quality applications in a straightforward manner without infringing on someone else's copyrights or defrauding users based on bogus claims.

Anyone with a little time and programming knowledge can produce Android applications. That opens up the mobile phone to a whole new world. Users in specific industries can create applications that others in those industries will find useful. Similarly, users with specific interests can create applications useful to people who share those interests. And anyone who creates an application can build it from predesigned open source components that have been tried and tested. The result is better, more useful applications for users.

How It All Comes Together

Suddenly, you have the perfect operating system for mobile devices. And you have a community of developers ready and willing to create applications for the device. Now all you need is the device. That's how the T-Mobile G1—the first Android-based device—came onto the scene.

The G1 is a simple device that many criticized for not being sleek or flashy when it first hit the market. However, what the device lacks in fashion, it makes up for in usability, as you'll learn in this book. Still, it didn't take T-Mobile and HTC long to rectify the mistake. Less than a year after the release of the G1 a sleeker, sexier Android-based phone—the T-Mobile myTouch—made its appearance. The myTouch has all the great functionality of its predecessor, just in a prettier package.

Part I: Devices

The book is divided into three sections, each devoted to a different aspect of the Android-based device. Part I, "Devices," focuses on the devices and walks you through how to use them. This part is similar to the owner's manual, but with tips, tricks, and observations thrown in to help you get the most out of whichever device you own.

Part I is a short section of the book—only three chapters. In Chapter 1, "The Theory of the Android Phone," you'll learn a lot more about the theory of the Google phone and how it was created. This is your history lesson. This chapter also includes useful information such as user statistics, in case you're interested in developing applications and want to know what your market might look like.

In Chapter 2, "Getting to Know Android Phones," you really get to know your new device. This chapter walks you through the basics of using the phone, including an introduction to hardware and preinstalled applications on the device.

Chapter 3, "Basic Use of Your Android Phone," covers how to use the basic functions of the phone, such as making calls and sending messages. By the time you're finished with this chapter, you'll know how to use those functions like a pro. You might already know how to use these functions, but we encourage you to skim through all the chapters in this part anyway. You might discover tips and tricks, shortcuts, or useful capabilities that you didn't already know about.

Part II: The Applications

You may have found the device lacking in visual appeal, but this area of the Android phone will likely impress you. The preinstalled applications and other applications available through the Android Market are much richer and more useful than applications for other types of mobile devices.

Each chapter in this section focuses on a different application or set of applications that is considered a *core application.* These core applications are available on all Android-based devices. You don't have to use them, but because they're either Google based or designed specifically for Android, these applications will probably give you the best experiences. Part II, "The Applications," covers these core applications:

- **Chapter 4, "Core Applications"**—This chapter walks you through using several core applications on the Android-based device, including Contacts, Calendar, Alarm, Calculator, and Camera. This information includes not only the basics on how to use these applications, but also tips and tricks that will make you a power user.

- **Chapter 5, "Going Online"**—Because surfing the Web is the number one reason people seek out web-enabled mobile devices, here you'll find everything you need to know about using the installed web browser. That includes information about controls and settings, and alternatives, just in case you don't care for the browser installed on the device.

- **Chapter 6, "Email Anywhere"**—The Android-based device gives you access to two types of email programs: Gmail and everything else. If you're a Gmail user, you'll find that the Android-based device makes your messaging experiences much richer. But not everyone loves Gmail, so you do have other options. This chapter walks you through using both methods for accessing your email from your mobile device.

- **Chapter 7, "Getting Around with GPS and Google Maps"**—One of the most anticipated features of the Android-based device is Google Maps and the available GPS integration. This chapter outlines the capabilities of those features and walks you through all the controls for those capabilities.

■ **Chapter 8, "Breaking Boredom with Entertainment Options"**—No device is complete without a good set of entertainment applications. Many people are completely addicted to music, so, of course, there's a music application. And without YouTube, many of us would waste away to nothing, so the device also has a YouTube application. You can even get games and other applications through the Android Market. This chapter shows you how to use all these functions.

■ **Chapter 9, "Adding Applications to Your Device"**—In addition to the core applications, you'll probably want to give your Android-based device other capabilities. Maybe you want to take notes, record reminders, or level the picture you're hanging. You can add these capabilities by downloading applications from the Android Market. This chapter walks you through finding, installing, and rating third-party applications.

Android is really more of an experience than a platform. You can do so much more with a mobile device than just make calls and send messages. Android opens the door for limitless possibilities in the mobile arena, and we look forward to seeing how the whole experience grows in the coming months and years.

Part III: The Android Platform

The final part of this book covers creating applications for your Android phone. If you don't know anything about programming concepts or JavaScript, you might want to find out about those before you tackle this section of the book. At a minimum, you need to understand the principles of programming and the basics of Java.

If you have those qualifications, however, you can write your own Android-based applications. In this section of the book, we show you how. Don't worry if you've never written an application for a mobile phone. We walk you through the process from beginning to end.

In Chapter 10, "Getting to Know Android," you'll find a detailed introduction to the Android platform. This includes everything you need to know about how Android works before you begin to create applications based on the Android platform.

Then in Chapter 11, "Developing Native Android Apps," you'll move into the basics of creating mobile web applications. This chapter includes information about how web content is designed differently for Android and tips on how to create mobile applications that perform well.

You really get into the meat of developing applications for Android in Chapter 12, "Developing Mobile Web Applications." This chapter covers topics such as getting started with the Android SDK and using the necessary add-ons during the programming process. Before you finish reading this chapter, you'll have a complete development environment in which to build your applications.

With the development environment in place, you can actually start developing applications. Chapter 13, "Advanced Android Apps," introduces you to some of the most advanced Android applications for your device.

Creating applications for the Android-based device is exciting. Because you can build on open source components, you don't need to waste time rewriting code that already exists. That means you can spend more time creating functions within applications that people will truly find useful. Even if you think that the application you're designing will be useful only to you, consider sharing it on the Android Market. You might be surprised by how many other people have the same problems or needs.

Appendixes

Finally, you'll find two appendixes in this book. Appendix A, "Troubleshooting," is divided into three sections: troubleshooting device issues, troubleshooting application issues, and troubleshooting design issues. You'll find questions and answers for some of the most common issues that we encountered when using the device and applications and during programming. This is by no means a complete list of the problems you might encounter, but we hope that the answers here will help if you do encounter problems.

You'll likely use Appendix B, "G1 Keyboard Shortcuts," more than any other part of the book. This appendix lists the different keyboard shortcuts that you can use with the applications and features of the Android-based device. You might want to copy this reference tool and post it in the areas where you use the device most often. They're simple shortcuts, but they'll reduce the amount of time (and the number of key presses or touches) you'll need to access some of the applications and features you use most often.

Special Features

As you read through the chapters, you'll come across a set of special features that are designed to help you pull out important bits of information about the subjects we cover:

Geek Speak—Jargon is frustrating. We do our best to avoid jargon whenever possible, but sometimes it's not possible. These boxes define jargon words in clear language.

 No Joke—Be careful! You could damage your device or lose data in some places. These boxes offer cautions to help you avoid damaging the device, application, or data as you work through the steps in the book.

 Yellow Box—In the Google culture, the Yellow Box is a search appliance that leads to additional information. Our Yellow Box performs the same function. If you need more information—a useful tip or trick or even a few sentences of deeper information to clarify a concept—you can find it using the Yellow Box.

Privileged Information Sidebar—Sometimes really interesting information relates to the topic at hand, but it's not completely relevant to the steps we're walking you through or the information we're giving you. Maybe the additional information makes it easier for you to understand and use a component. For those cases, a sidebar provides the privileged information you need, or at least a pointer to get you headed in the right direction.

Each of these features contains information that makes this book more useful to you, so, keep your eyes open for them.

Who Should Read This Book?

If you've picked up the book and gotten this far into the Introduction, it's a good bet that you're part of the audience for the book. We're writing for both beginners and intermediate users. Beginners will find all the information that they need to get started using the Android-based device, and intermediate users will find additional tips, tricks, and information on programming Android applications.

If you're an advanced user, you'll probably find only review information in these pages, but an occasional review is good. As we advance into the upper levels of the user kingdom, we often forget some of the basic and simple uses, practices, and applications. Even advanced users might benefit from quickly skimming these pages.

Our goal is to help readers use their Android-based device to the fullest extent possible. We want you to be as excited about Android and Android devices as we are, so we've worked hard to pass on all the information that we can to help you make the most of them.

Of course, things change. By the time this book hits the shelves, many changes will have occurred that we can't cover here. We've set up a website to help you track those changes. The website www.WebGeeksGuide.com includes a blog with regular updates about products, devices, and applications. You'll also find additional training materials as they become available for new fea-tures and applications. And, of course, we welcome your comments about this or any of the other Web Geek's Guides on the website. Use the Contact Us link as often as you want.

Okay, we've blabbered on long enough about basics and features of the book. Let's get on with the book itself. We hope that you find the information you seek and that we've presented it in a way that makes it easy for you to use. Thanks for reading!

Devices

In this part:

- The Theory of the Android Phone
- Getting to Know Android Phones
- Basic Use of Your Android Phone

Internet buzz about the Android platform has intensified since the first mention of it slipped out in July 2005, when Google acquired a small company named Android. A year later, amid cries that Android could be the best mobile platform ever, the first Android-based phone was released. And here we are today.

This part of the book looks at some of the (short) history of the Android platform. Chapter 1, "The Theory of the Android Phone," lays down the foundation for why Google even got involved in the mobile platform.

The next two chapters—Chapter 2, "Getting to Know Android Phones," and Chapter 3, "Basic Use of Your Android Phone," are just quick getting started chapters. If you've already been playing with your Android Phone, you may not need this information. It makes a good reference, though, if it's been a while since you started using the phone. And who knows? You might find a trick or two that you didn't know about.

If you're new to the Android Phone, this is your Quick Start Guide. The chapters offer a balance of useful text instruction and easy to understand images so you'll quickly be able to walk through all the basic functions of the phone.

Let's jump right in.

1

The Theory of the Android Phone

Although it might seem that Google Android popped up out of left field, that's not entirely true. Well, maybe it's a little true, because Google didn't actually concept Android. Let's start with the birthing of the idea.

Believe it or not, Android started as the brain child of Andy Rubin. He concepted Android as an *open source* mobile platform that would bring the mobile industry out of the Paleolithic era into modern society.

Open source is a method of developing computer applications and programs so that the source code is readily available. Essentially, it opens up application development for collaboration from a wide variety of programmers of differing skill levels. Many believe that this is the most efficient method of creating the best possible programs and applications. You'll learn a lot more about open source in Part III, "The Android Platform," when we get into tweaking and creating apps for Android.

The mobile industry has been hopelessly tied to more traditional thought processes about how people use phones—that is, phones with wires and cords. Before the advent of the mobile phone, people had to use phones in an area no larger than their home or office.

Rubin understood that today's mobile phone user has different needs. He designed a mobile platform that would enable any programmer to write any application for the mobile phone platform, to meet the demand of mobile phone users. In 2005, he went to Google looking for backing.

When Rubin approached Google, he wasn't looking for funding. He was looking for a seal of approval. Rubin had already discovered that Google has long coattails for a mobile company: He used Google as the default search application on the T-Mobile Sidekick (shown in Figure 1.1). The Sidekick took off better than anyone had imagined. And with Google as the phone's default search engine, suddenly people were using the mobile web.

FIGURE 1.1

With Google as the default search engine, the T-Mobile Sidekick was more popular with users than the creators imagined it could be.

When Rubin went searching for Google's approval, he got an offer that he couldn't walk away from. Google offered to pay Rubin around $50 million for Android and agreed to put him in charge of the Android project. Rubin accepted, and the rest of the story is told in the melding of platforms, applications, and the right devices.

The Melding of Google Mobile and Android

Long before Android came into the picture, the leaders at Google knew that mobility would eventually become a large part of the business. No, Google founders Larry Page and Sergey Brin are not clairvoyant. But they do understand how people communicate, and it didn't take an astrophysicist (although either of them could easily have been astrophysicists, had they been so inclined) to figure it out. All either man had to do was live a normal life, connected to their cellphones, as they surely often are. And if that wasn't enough to convince them, surely a glance around the Google-plex would. No doubt all Google employees use their cellphones much like a lifeline, even on the übertech campus.

Fortunately, Brin and Page aren't dumb. Their first foray into the mobile world was with the release of Google SMS in late 2004. Less than a year later, in June 2005, Google Mobile Search (shown in Figure 1.2) was released; Gmail for Mobile (shown in Figure 1.3) followed a few months later, in December 2005. Brin and Page just had to figure out how to make it all work for Google and for users. That took a little longer.

So when Rubin brought the idea of Android to the Google team, Google knew the company wanted—maybe even needed—to be involved in the project. Google already had its hands in mobile technology but was exploring how to best take advantage of it.

The release of Google Chrome barely a month before the release of the first Android-based phone added another piece to the puzzle. *Googlites* had been working on an open source web browser that would enable each instance of the browser to run separately, to make the best use of available resources and to increase the security of browsing the Web.

Googlites are people who work with Google. They are also sometimes called *Googlers*.

FIGURE 1.2

Google Mobile Search enables users to search from wherever they are, using their cellular connection. You can use Mobile Search on any Internet-enabled phone.

FIGURE 1.3

Gmail Mobile gives users email access directly from their mobile device. You can use Gmail Mobile on any Internet-enabled phone.

How does that translate into mobile browsing? Both efficient resource usage and browser security are requirements for browsing the Web on a 2x3 screen. First, mobile phones don't have the processing power that desktop and laptop computers have. The processor is much smaller, storage space is limited, and the whole browsing experience is different.

Having a browser that starts each new web-based application as a new page enabled Google to create a browser that operated quickly on limited resources but still shared resources, where possible, to make pages and applications load faster. That's an essential feature when you're talking about browsing the Web over mobile phone signals because a mobile phone's data transmission frequency is not quite as fast as the frequency over which broadband Internet users are accustomed to receiving web data.

Security was also a major concern. Today's mobile phones are becoming more vulnerable to hackers trying to spread viruses and phishing for personal information to be used in identity theft and credit card fraud. Each instance of the Google Chrome browser runs independently of all the others; therefore, one affected window does not affect another. Closing down the affected window efficiently ends whatever processes are taking place, ensuring that malware-ridden processes are closed completely.

In the mobile phone environment, this means that an open window on your phone is only partly as dangerous as it was before. Yes, the dangers still exist in that window, but when you click a link and move to a second window, that second window is free of the same malware. This also means that closing one window effectively shuts down whatever problems might exist within that window.

In short, independent instances of windows make it much harder (though not impossible) for hackers to create a spoofed web that tricks you into believing you're entering your personal, credit, or banking information.

Chrome is a browser that's built for computer users, but Chrome is built using the same technology and theories that the Android web browser is built upon. You can easily see that Google is striving to take advantage of the opportunities that mobile web users provide.

LEARNING MORE ABOUT GOOGLE CHROME

We don't have nearly enough room to cover all the features of Google Chrome. For example, Google Chrome is open source software, which means that users can change and tweak it to meet their needs. Already, some companies have adopted Chrome as their internal browser and

1

tweaked it not only to show their company logo, but also to work specifically with some of their internal processes.

If you're so inclined, and have the right skill set, Chrome is a great browser to support your take on customization. You can learn more about how to do that in the second book in the Geek Series, *The Geek's Guide to Google Chrome* (ISBN 0789739739, Que Publishing, 2009).

Don't think there are opportunities there? Think again. Look at the Apple iPhone. On Christmas 2007, thousands of new iPhone users received their first iPhone as a gift. Do you know what their first activity was after getting online? Searching Google. Really. At the time, the iPhone accounted for less than 5% of all the smart phones in the world. But on that day, it accounted for more traffic to the Google website than all the other mobile platforms combined.

The brains at Google being brains, they understood this day was coming—and they acquired Android. They continued to build out applications, such as Gmail, Google Earth, Google Docs, and YouTube, that would work well in mobile environments. It's essential to have a little foresight about these things. Mobile isn't just a cool new technology for the geeks among us. It's a whole new way of living life.

Today's Internet Society

Part of what is driving the dramatic increase in mobile connectedness and functionality is the shaping of an Internet society that removes many barriers that previously kept people corralled to their local areas. A few years ago, the Internet was just beginning to become part of our culture. It started out as a method that scholar geeks used to transfer information to other scholar geeks. Then lesser geeks like us started using it and found a few neat features that proved truly useful—email, instant messaging, and news services. The Internet was cool but still infantile by today's standards.

And what exactly are today's standards? It hasn't been scientifically proven yet, but I'm pretty sure today's kids are born with an inherent understanding of the Internet. And now the interconnectedness of it removes all boundaries.

Don't believe me? Hand any 6-year-old an Internet-enabled cellphone, and in 5 minutes he'll be on MySpace or Facebook posting bulletins about how to build a Lego charger for your Nintendo handheld gaming system. It's true … well, okay, maybe it's a bit of a stretch, but not by much.

Yellow Box

The Lego charger really does exist. If you're looking for a neat science project, you can learn more about creating a Lego charger for a variety of devices at either of these two URLs:

www.instructables.com/id/EE0I17GSI0EUAB84WC/

http://gremspot.blogspot.com/2005/03/lego-charger-cradle-for-nintendo-ds.html

The point is that the Internet is a way of life now, and the Internet on a cellphone is quickly becoming part of that way of life. Being connected to friends and family, no matter where they are, is nearly as important as breathing. The social aspect of the Internet is huge, but there's more to it than that.

It's also about information—having the information you want or need in a format that's easy to access *the moment you need it.* That is where the Internet and cellphones come together as a catalyst for today's Internet society.

Nokia released the first Internet-enabled cellphone in 1996. But true mobile Internet service didn't come along until 1999, and then it was only in Japan. From 1999 to today, the mobile Internet has taken over—many experts estimate that the iPhone has knocked down yet another Internet barrier. Instead of purchasing Internet service for laptop and desktop computers, many people, especially in lower income brackets, are skipping wired Internet altogether and going straight to mobile Internet for email access and web surfing.

This makes sense from a financial standpoint. You could buy a computer and pay $600–$1,000 (or more) for it, and then subscribe to an Internet service for around $25–$50 per month, and still pay for your cellphone and cellphone service (because without a cellphone, life ceases to exist). Or you could skip the extra cost, stick with the cellphone, and add a measly $25–$35 per month to your bill for unlimited Internet service. For those whose interest is purely in Internet and email access at the least expensive price, the mobile Internet is an economical solution.

Despite the overwhelming adoption of mobile Internet, however, challenges still exist, and that's where Google stepped into the picture with the Android operating system.

Mobile Internet needs to be more functional. To date, only a small percentage of websites have mobile versions of their sites that people can view comfortably from the tiny display of a mobile phone.

Bringing It All Together

Now mobility and usability need to come together. That brings us back to Google Android. Google is known as the "king of search," but what might not be so obvious (and that's probably a good thing) is that Google also rules when it comes to usability.

If you didn't recognize that, it's because Google has nailed usability so well that you don't even think about it. Most Google applications are pretty easy to use. Minimal time is required to get up-to-speed on them, and users only really need to ask for help with activities that power users might want to do.

That applies to Google's mobile applications as well. Using Gmail Mobile or Google Mobile Search is just as easy as using Gmail or Google Search on your computer. Google has even taken it one step further to make it easier to use some of those applications on a mobile platform. For example, Google Mobile also has a voice capability that enables you to search for places, events, and other information by stating what you're looking for.

The challenge, of course, is making the Internet usable on a small-form factor, in the ways people want to use it. That means appealing to different audiences using different devices.

Making Devices Usable

Around 200 models of Internet-capable phones are currently available on the market. Of those devices, many are small, with screens that are about an inch and a half square. The most usable devices, however, have screens that are roughly 2 inches by 3 inches—think of the Android-enabled T-Mobile G1, shown in Figure 1.4.

In addition to the device, there's functionality to take into consideration. Surfing the Web on a mobile phone is more labor intensive than surfing the Web on a computer. A user might have to type 10–25 characters into a regular web browser to perform a search, for example, but a user searching from a mobile device might require as many as 40 keystrokes to type those same 10–25 characters. Because of the way the keyboards are set up on a mobile phone, users also spend more time typing those keystrokes.

Now, many of the Internet-enabled mobile phones that are hitting the market today are designed to take advantage of mobile web surfing. New device features, such as touch screens, full QWERTY keyboards, and even more intuitive voice commands, are becoming standard features on phones. Users demand more usability, and device manufacturers are providing it.

FIGURE 1.4

The T-Mobile G1 belongs to a class of mobile phones that is designed for mobile Internet usability.

Adding Software Applications to the Mix

In addition to the functionality of the phone, the software and applications that are installed on or available for an Internet-enabled mobile phone are a factor in the usability of the device. But these applications must appeal to two distinct groups of users: those raised on the Internet and mobile devices and the rest of us, who use the mobile web a little differently. Those raised on the Internet and mobile devices tend to use those devices as a means of extending their community. That means they're not only part of productivity, but they're also part of a lifestyle. Those who weren't necessarily raised with a mobile device in our hands are typically more interested in finding information, staying connected to home and work, and accomplishing something. We don't have time to use the mobile web as a social network, but we also don't have time not to. We're busy, and our idea of mobility is being able to accomplish more during times when we were out of the loop in the past.

Mobile application designers have to bring applications to the market that reach both groups of people. It's a challenge. Working in a smaller form factor means understanding the audience you're trying to reach. It means spending time to find out what a specific segment of the audience wants and needs from an application. It also means understanding that sometimes there's a crossover from one group to the next.

That's what Google does best. Google has spent a lot of money learning how and why users use the Web. Studying different age groups, hiring the best and brightest minds in the world, and keeping an open mind about what's coming next has helped Google tap into a market that's set to explode in ways that we're only beginning to understand.

And now Google is translating all that to the mobile platform with Google Android. The phone is cool, but it's really just a device—one that will change rapidly and repeatedly. One device will lead to a better device, which will lead to a better one, and so on until the whole factor has changed significantly.

What really makes the mobile web usable is the applications that are available on the devices. Some of these applications come preinstalled on the device. Others are add-ons that users can install and uninstall at will, based on their current needs. And that's where we are now.

We have some of the best devices that the mobile market has ever seen, now available to users. The applications that make those devices truly useful are growing rapidly. Google Android is designed to be a platform that makes those applications grow faster, better, and stronger than anything that we've seen in the past.

Through the open source nature of Android, developers around the world are building applications for Android-based phones. And because it is open source, those applications are improved and added to on a daily basis. The variety is monstrous. From productivity applications such as spreadsheets and calculators to purely social applications such as Twitter and blogger aids, endless possibilities exist for every type of user. That's the promise of Android: to make the Web usable for everyone. Google seems to be successfully keeping this promise.

Closing the Door

In this chapter, you've learned how Android was concepted and how it became Google Android. You've also seen the usability of the mobile Internet and the current challenges to its adoption. But Google has met those challenges well with Google Android. Now it's time to learn more about the device: the T-Mobile G1 and the T-Mobile myTouch, also known as the HTC Magic. Keep reading. In the next chapter, you'll get a quick tour of the devices and their features and capabilities.

Getting to Know Android Phones

W hen Google introduced Android, it was certain that a device that operated on Android follow close behind. Then T-Mobile jumped on board and the official announcement came: The new "Google Phone" would soon be released for the world to see.

As with nearly every device announcement these days, that announcement brought false information and speculation about what the device would look like, what it would include, and what it would do. Then came the delays. Initially expected to be available during the first or second quarter of 2008, the phone was delayed to the third quarter of 2008.

On October 22, 2008, the first "Google Phone" finally made its long-awaited appearance. Lots of flourish and hype preceded the device unveiling, and plenty of good and bad reviews followed it. People loved the full keyboard, but hated the fact that the device is T-Mobile specific. They loved the Google apps and hated them. It was uncertain how the phone would go over with the public.

Then the device—called the T-Mobile G1—hit the market, and sales proved that people loved it.

The T-Mobile G1 is a good device—solidly built and intuitive to use. It's also the first device to feature Google's Android platform. More Android devices will come in the future, but this one has already earned a place in people's hearts, so let's learn a little more about it.

The T-Mobile G1

If you're just getting the T-Mobile G1, you'll find that it's fairly easy to use. You need to figure out just a few buttons, shown in Figure 2.1. Most of the functionality is built into the touch screen capabilities. (If you already have a T-Mobile G1 or myTouch, you've probably figured out the phones, so feel free to skip ahead to the second part of the book where we cover applications, or even Part III where we cover Android.)

The T-Mobile G1 is shipped with everything you need to use it, including the following:

- 1 Gb Micro SD Card (4 Gb for the myTouch)
- AC power cord
- Stereo Headphones
- Computer sync cable (USB)
- Soft cover/pouch
- Battery

FIGURE 2.1

The T-Mobile G1 has a few buttons and a slide-out QWERTY keyboard.

One thing you won't find in the box is a car charger. Although this would be a nice addition, one rarely comes with any phone. Fortunately, the G1 charges through a USB cable, so if you have a car charger with a USB slot, you're in business.

The Buttons

The T-Mobile G1 has a very Spartan appearance. On the front of the device are five simple buttons and a trackball, shown in Figure 2.2. Table 2.1 explains the buttons and their functions.

The buttons control more functions than you might think because you use two types of presses for different functions. The first press is a normal key press that you use to access the main function of the button. The second press lasts a couple seconds longer; for some buttons, that long press brings up additional menus or functions.

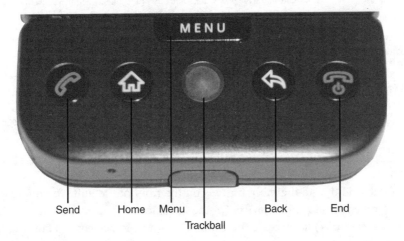

Send   Home   Menu   Back   End
               Trackball

FIGURE 2.2

The buttons on the G1 are easy to find and the functions are fairly obvious.

Table 2.1   The G1 Buttons and Their Functions

Button Name	Function
Send Key	Press to begin a call from a highlighted number in the Contacts list or on a web page. Long press to open the Voice Dialer. Press to open the call log. Press to answer an incoming call while on another call. Press to display current call information.
Home Key	Press to return to main menu screen from any application. Long press to open a menu of the last six programs you've accessed (called the Applications window).
Menu Key	Press to open a menu of available commands on any page. Press once then long press to flash a menu of shortcuts on pages where shortcuts are available. Press twice to wake the phone from sleep mode and unlock the screen.
Trackball	Navigate and scroll pages, links, and other functionality within a page. Moves selection up, down, right, and left. Press to select an option or click a link.
Back Key	Press to move back to the previous screen from any location. Press to dismiss a dialog box or menu and return to the previous screen.
End Key	Press to end a call. Press to send the phone to sleep. Long press to bring up a menu that allows you to enable or disable silent mode or to power off the phone. When the phone is off, press to turn it on.

In addition to the main buttons on the front of the unit, you'll find a button on each side of the device. On the left side is a volume button (see Figure 2.3). Press up (+) to increase the volume, down (-) to decrease it. Pressing the button during an active call increases or decreases the call volume. Pressing the button when no call is active increases or decreases the ring volume; within applications, the same button controls the application volume.

The button on the right side of the unit, shown in Figure 2.4, controls the 3.2 megapixel camera. To activate the camera, start at the Home screen (that's the main screen) and then press and hold the camera capture button. (If you try to activate it from any other screen or application, the camera won't open.) Then press the button again to take pictures.

FIGURE 2.3

The volume button, on the left side of the unit.

FIGURE 2.4

The camera button activates the camera and takes pictures.

 Be warned: The camera application that comes installed on the G1 is a little slow. You'll experience a 2- to 3-second delay from the time you press the button until the time the shutter actually opens and closes to capture the shot. If you're not patient, you could end up with some blurry photos.

You can also press the camera button halfway down when taking pictures to prefocus the picture so that it shoots faster. However, the button is difficult to push, so doing this can shake the phone and result in blurry pictures. Sometimes it's smarter to press the button completely and then hold the phone steady while the camera focuses and shoots.

One way that issue has been addressed was in the update to the Android 1.5 firmware. The update included a new on-screen button for the camera. Once you've framed your shot, simply touch the on-screen button to take the picture. A mini-preview window also appears on the screen to display the last picture taken.

The G1 also has a full QWERTY keyboard, shown in Figure 2.5. The keyboard is backlit, making it easier to use in low-light conditions, and the buttons are raised enough that they make a satisfying click when pressed. People with large hands may have trouble using the keyboard because the keys are small and fairly close together. A good way to get around this is to use a soft-touch stylus to press the keys—a stylus also works well on the touch screen of the device.

FIGURE 2.5

The G1 has a full slide-out QWERTY keyboard for typing messages, numbers, and other data.

ONE TOUCH DOES NOT EQUAL ANOTHER

If you're new to using a touch-capable device, you might not realize that one type of touch device isn't necessarily the same as the next. In the past, touch-screen PDAs and phones could be used with a stylus, a pen-like device with a plastic tip instead of an ink tip. The stylus made touching (or clicking) the smaller options easier and could be used for input, including handwriting recognition.

The cool thing about the touch capabilities of earlier devices, called *resistive touch*, is that they worked based on the amount of pressure placed on the screen of the device, so you could use a specialized stylus, a pen cap, or even your fingernail.

However, the touch capabilities of the G1 are *capacitive touch* capabilities, which means that the screen reacts with the electrical impulses in your fingers. In other words, a normal stylus won't work with the T-Mobile G1; you must use a specialized stylus.

Fortunately, capacitive styli are easy to find and cost $5–$20, depending on where you get them.

Another feature added with the Android 1.5 update is the on-screen keyboard. The keyboard, similar to that which can be found on an iPhone or iPod touch, gives you most of the controls that can be found on the slide-out keyboard. A few of the keys (most notably the Menu key and the Search key) are missing, but it's otherwise fully functional.

A nice feature of the on-screen keyboard is that you can add sound and vibration to confirm keytouches or you can turn the on-screen keyboard off entirely if you don't want to use it. You'll find these controls by pressing the Menu key. Then select **Settings > Locale & text**. Deselect the first instance of **Android Keyboard** to turn the keyboard off, or touch the second instance of **Android Keyboard** to adjust the settings to your liking. You may have to play with them some to find a combination that you're comfortable using.

Screen Icons

The G1 is a touch-screen phone, which is why the device itself has so few buttons. Most of the functionality is available through the three-panel touch screen. Most of your interaction with the phone takes place on the main touch screen. You can add to or remove the basic icons as desired.

Standard on the main touch screen are five icons and a clock:

 myFaves—The My Faves icon is specific to the T-Mobile service, so if you're using the G1 on another service, you won't see this icon. T-Mobile users know that this represents the people listed in the My Faves category of the phone. You're allowed a specific number of My Faves, depending on the plan you've selected with T-Mobile, whom you can call and receive calls from for free.

Dialer—Here you access your onscreen dial pad, your call log, your contacts, and your favorites.

Contacts—This takes you directly to the Contacts screen within the dialer. From this screen, you'll see a list of contacts that you can select, edit, change, or add to.

Browser—The browser enables you to surf the Web on the phone. When you touch this icon, the web browser opens to the page you've set as your home page or to the default home page, if you haven't changed the settings.

Maps—Maps were a big selling point for Google when the G1 was announced. When you touch the Maps icon, you activate a Google Maps application that enables you to use GPS or Wi-Fi to find maps, get directions, and even locate yourself.

In addition to this main screen, you have a right screen and a left screen. The right screen contains the Google search box, so you can search without having to launch your web browser. The left screen is blank except for the background. You can access these screens by sweeping your finger to the right or left across the face of the phone.

On either of these screens, you can add icons for the applications that you access most frequently. Chapter 3, "Basic Use of Your Android Phone," includes instructions for how to add and remove icons on any of the three screens.

On the main screen of the device, you'll also see a small gray arrow either at the bottom of the screen or on the right side of the screen, if you've changed the view to Landscape mode (see Figure 2.6).

Yellow Box

Another neat feature that was included with the Android 1.5 update is the ability to use the accelerometer to automatically change your screen orientation. Just by flipping your phone you can move between portrait and landscape viewing modes. To enable or disable this feature go to **Menu > Settings > Sound & display** then select or deselect **Orientation**.

This menu indicates that you can choose among other application options. You can touch and drag the arrow to open the menu to explore additional program options. When you're done, touch or touch and drag the arrow to close the menu.

Menu Button

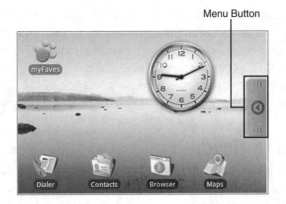

FIGURE 2.6

The arrow at the bottom or side of the screen indicates a menu of further application options.

The top of the screen also shows a status bar (see Figure 2.7), where you can see icons indicating the status of your service. These icons include indicators for wireless service, cellular network service, time, and battery life. Other indicators appear in the status bar as they are needed, including GPS and Bluetooth indicators, missed call icons, email icons, appointment and text message notifications, and download and installation indicators when you're adding new applications to the phone.

Status Bar

FIGURE 2.7

The status bar at the top of the Home screen gives you a quick look at phone and application status.

The status bar offers than meets the eye, however. At any time, you can expand the status bar to take a closer look at notifications by simply placing your finger on the status bar and then sweeping down toward the bottom of the page. This opens the bar so that you can see and clear notifications that appear. When you're done, close the status bar by touching the small dot on the bottom of the page and dragging upward, or by pressing the Back key.

The T-Mobile myTouch

The newest Android offering as of this writing is the T-Mobile myTouch, shown in Figure 2.8. This second generation Android phone is only slightly different from the T-Mobile G1. Most notably, there is no slide-out keyboard on the myTouch. That means the device is slightly smaller, a little curvier, and a whole lot sexier. But it doesn't mean you're losing functionality because the keyboard is missing. It just means the device is designed a little differently.

FIGURE 2.8

The T-Mobile myTouch is the second generation Android phone with a sleek new look.

Remember earlier in this chapter when we mentioned that there are a couple of keys missing from the on-screen keyboard? Well, on the myTouch, they've just been relocated to the handset, as shown in Figure 2.9. The trackball is still in place, but surrounding it there are now six keys on the handset: Home, Menu, Back, Search, Send, and End. The keys perform all the same functions, they've just been slightly rearranged.

The Search and Menu keys are now on the device

FIGURE 2.9

Because there is no slide-out keyboard on the myTouch, there are a couple extra buttons on the front.

There is also no camera button on the side of the device. Instead, you'll have to access the camera using the Camera icon and the on-screen buttons designed to take pictures (so, that's why they were included in Android 1.5!). The camera, incidentally, is a 3.5 megapixel camera, but there's still no flash.

The only other real differences between the G1 and the myTouch are internal. The myTouch is designed to process a little more efficiently (read faster) than the G1. A new group of applications, called the "T-Mobile App Pack," will allow users to interact more closely with T-Mobile. There's also an application, called Sherpa, included that is a presence-type application, meaning it can make more of the things that you do with your phone convenient to the time and place you're using the phone.

Of course, the myTouch is also a little more customizable from an appearance standpoint. A variety of new casing colors and designs is available, as are skins for the newest member of the T-Mobile family. A few different accessories are also included with the myTouch. A zippered case is among them, which we're assuming is in response to the horrible case that came with the G1.

Overview of Software and Applications

Now that you know a little about using your phone, let's take a quick look at the software and applications installed on the Android phone. Most of what makes Android phones such ground-breaking devices is the software. Sure, the devices are pretty sweet, but other touch phones do as much or more than the Android phones.

The operating system, Android, really sets the devices apart from other devices. We touched on Android a little in Chapter 1, "The Theory of the Android Phone," so you should be familiar with its history—but there's much more to it than just history.

The concept of Android is important—along with its capabilities, of course. When Google decided to invest in Android, it formed the Open Handset Alliance (OHA), a group of 47 mobile device manufacturers including Google. The OHA is dedicated to making mobile devices that are cheaper, easier to use, and more functional—which is precisely why it chose to invest time and resources into the development of Android.

Android in Brief

We stated earlier that Android is an operating system, but it's really more than that. It's a stack of technology built specifically for mobile devices that includes an operating system, middleware, and key applications.

This stack of software includes everything from the framework to specialized pieces of software such as a virtual machine that facilitates the optimization of memory and hardware resources to connectivity technologies such as Bluetooth and Wi-Fi.

The whole package is built on a Linux kernel that supports customizations and changes as developers improve on the applications they're building for the platform. This makes the Android platform different from the platform on which other mobile devices are based because developers can take advantage of all the phone's capabilities.

For example, developers have created a social media application that enables members to track the actual physical movements of other members using the GPS capabilities of the device. When two users who are connected are within a specified radius of each other, they can receive notifications and set up an in-person meeting, if they like.

This illustrates another capability of the Android system that other platforms don't have: Android allows multitasking to use multiple apps at once. Thus, developers can design applications to take advantage of the full range of technology built into the phone.

The idea with Android is to give developers the freedom they need to create applications that are truly useful in the moment, instead of being useful only when it's dictated that those applications should be. For example, using Android, application developers can add modules to applications to make them useful when you're performing a specific task at work, as well as when you're performing that task at home. However, you can keep those instances separate, so there's no confusion between work and home activities.

This is a genius idea. Why force people to use applications that they might or might not find useful? Why not allow those same people to create their own useful applications?

Granted, not everyone has the skill set to create applications for a mobile device, but you might be surprised by how many actually have those skills. Many people have developed an understanding of programming languages, even if it's not their primary career.

Because Android applications are based on Java and all the tools to create the applications are free in the Android SDK, anyone with the time and inclination can create applications for the device. What's more, because so many people are creating these applications and sharing the code—because it *is* open source—developers can apply the best parts of one application to another application, to create even richer applications.

Android also doesn't differentiate between core applications and third-party applications, so there are no blocks in the functionality that's available for any application from the Android Market. These applications perform on Android just like the applications that come preinstalled on the device.

Core Applications

The core applications that come installed on the Android phones are pretty basic applications. You'll find all the main functionality that you would expect to find with a smart phone, except perhaps a productivity suite of applications. The G1 has a full keyboard and both devices have on-screen keyboards, so that's one group of applications (at least, the document and spreadsheet portion) that you might expect to see. However, because Google makes those productivity applications available online, it's possible that the decision was that they wouldn't be needed directly on the device.

The only 18 listed applications originally installed give you access to most of the basic functions that you'll need:

- **Alarm Clock**—The alarm clock is responsible for the clock icon that you find on the Home screen. Within the application, you can set up to three alarms and choose from five styles of clocks to display when the alarm sounds. Note, however, that changing the alarm clock display does not change the clock display on the Home screen.

- **Amazon MP3**—The Amazon MP3 application takes you to a mobile version of the Amazon MP3 website, where you can browse, buy, and download music directly to the device. Chapter 8, "Breaking Boredom with Entertainment Options," contains more information about the specific capabilities of Android's music capabilities.

- **Browser**—The built-in web browser was developed using WebKit, the same platform used to build the Google Chrome browser. It's unique because it allows separate and multiple instances of web pages. That speeds browsing but also increases security because each instance is a contained browsing experience. This means that if you run into malware in one instance and close that browser page, other browser pages that you have open aren't affected. Each time a page is closed, that instance is closed completely and doesn't bleed over to any other open instances.

- **Calculator**—This is a basic, functional calculator. It's not scientific and it doesn't do anything fancy, but this is one of the most used items on my device. We're amazed by how much more often we use a calculator when we have one with us all the time.

- **Calendar**—The calendar is tied into Google Calendar. If you have a Google Calendar account, you can sync it with the calendar on the device. You can configure syncing to happen at whatever interval you find most useful. You can keep your calendars always in sync and you get reminders on your phone.

- **Camera**—The 3.2-megapixel camera built into the Android phones takes good-quality pictures, although it has a slight delay during the picture-taking process when the camera focuses. You'll improve your picture quality when you get accustomed to the delay.

- **Contacts**—Contacts are tied to your Gmail account, if you have one. When you change and update contacts on the device, the contacts on your Gmail account also are updated on the next sync of the device. The device has space for several numbers, email addresses, physical addresses, and a picture icon of the contact. In addition, you can set specific ringtones, add company information, or add notes about the contact.

- **Dialer**—This is the number pad from which you dial calls or enter numbers in response to automated call systems. You won't find anything special here, but it is a requirement for a phone.

- **Email**—You're not tied to Gmail with the Android phone (although that's probably the most useful email account you can have if you use an Android-based phone). You can set up any web-based email account within Android so that you can access your email wherever you are.

- **Gmail**—Gmail comes preloaded on the device, along with the email options just mentioned. If you have a Gmail account, you can simply sign in; then each time you receive a message, you're notified on the phone.

- **IM**—The instant-messaging application works with AIM, Google Talk, Windows Live Messenger, and Yahoo! Messenger. Sign in and you can receive your IMs wherever you happen to be.

- **Maps**—Google Maps has even more functionality on the Android phones. You can search maps, get directions, and use Street View for a street-level view of your destination. Of course, it's available only for places where web cams are active, but you might be surprised by just how many places that includes.

- **Market**—This is the Android Market connection. Through Android Market, you can download hundreds of other games and applications for your phone.

- **Messaging**—This text-messaging application enables you to send SMS or multimedia messages.

- **Music**—The music player on the Android phones is basic. You can add music via the Amazon MP3 app or by loading it to the MicroSD card. Then you can sort it by artist, album, song, or playlist using this application. When you find the song you're looking for, select it to play it through the built-in speakers or your headphones.

- **Settings**—You manage all your device settings from this application.
- **Voice Dialer**—You can dial the people in your contacts using voice commands. You can also access the Voice Dialer by pressing and holding the green Call button on the device.
- **YouTube**—Yep, this is YouTube built right into your phone. Just click the icon to go to the YouTube site, where you can browse, search, and play videos.

The core applications come preinstalled on all Android devices, but they're not the only available applications. A whole world of applications awaits you in the Android Market.

Third-Party Apps

Developers who have created applications for the Android platform release those applications in the Android Market. Google kicked off application development for Android with a Developer Challenge, which resulted in hundreds of application submissions for consideration.

A small handful of applications were chosen to compete. Among them were Cooking Capsules (a small app that connects to podcasts that teach users to cook specific dishes), EcoRio (an app that tracks your carbon footprint), and ShopSavvy (an application that scans bar codes and then compares them with prices on the Web to help users find the best price).

Those first few applications opened the door for hundreds of others in 13 categories:

- Communication
- Entertainment
- Finance
- Games
- Lifestyle
- Multimedia
- News and weather
- Productivity
- Reference
- Shopping
- Social
- Tools
- Travel

Demo software also constitutes a category, although demos are often included in the category where the application belongs. You'll also find a category for software libraries that developers use in conjunction with other applications. For example, this category includes a text-to-speech (TTS) engine used with various applications, including a mapping capability. With the mapping application, you simply speak the directions onto the map so that you don't have to keep looking at your phone while you're driving.

The software library is another way for developers to share common elements of applications. Several other applications use the TTS engine, so it's made available for everyone to use; individual developers don't have to duplicate it. This element also needs to be installed on the device only once; each application that needs it then can reach out to that single instance to access the application that's installed.

An astounding variety of third-party apps is available. Many developers have improved on core apps, adding functionality beyond just the basics; others have created completely new applications. For example, several applications have already been developed for health care professionals, construction workers, traveling businesspeople, and busy people like us who need to have their to-do list with them all the time.

And because Android is open source, developers will continue to develop specific third-party applications and release them in the Android Market. User popularity will also drive the type of applications that are released. Over time, the selection will continue to grow and the types of applications that are available for the device will likely meet just about any need that you can come up with. And if no application suits your needs, you can always create one.

You do need to have some programming knowledge to create apps. For that, turn to Part III, "The Android Platform."

Device Security

We've touched a little on security from the application standpoint. In the browser, especially, the Android-enabled phone provides more security than others. But what about the actual device security?

If you're worried about someone picking up your phone and going through the data that's on it, or if you're concerned about someone using information on your phone if it's lost or stolen, you have an option: You can lock the device using a lock pattern that you draw by connecting at least four and up to nine dots on a security screen, as shown in Figure 2.10.

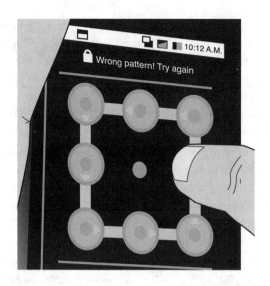

FIGURE 2.10

Create an unlock pattern that's specific to you to further protect your phone from prying strangers.

DEVICES AND YOUR PERSONAL SECURITY

Identity theft is the fastest-growing crime in the United States right now. More than 10 million people fell victim to identity theft in 2007. It's scary to think what a criminal can do to your credit, your identity, and your self-esteem with the right information.

Most people don't realize that they carry much of the information that's needed to steal an identity on a mobile device. If you have your personal information—name and address, telephone number, date of birth—on your device, you're opening the door for an identity thief. That little bit of information is all someone needs to get to a lot more.

Unfortunately, far too many people have that much information and far more (bookmarked accounts with saved usernames and passwords, for example) on their mobile device. If their phone is lost or stolen, they're at risk. Note that recycling or just plain tossing a phone out can also be just as dangerous.

We urge you to keep minimal personal information on your mobile devices. If you must keep personal information on them, practice safety. Keep the phone on you at all time. Never carry it in your purse with your wallet. Don't leave it in the car to be stolen. And always lock the device.

Identity theft is a crime that can take months to years to discover, and by that time, the damage may already be done. What's more, it can cost you hundreds or thousands of dollars to clear up the damage (assuming that you get it cleared up at all) and take more than 600 hours of your time. Be cautious.

And if you really like a good, scary story, check out *The Truth About Identity Theft* by Jim Stickley. This book walks you through the truths about identity theft that you might not know. You'll certainly be able to better protect yourself when you've finished reading it.

To set the lock pattern for your phone, follow these steps:

1. From the **Home** screen, touch the **Menu** button and select **Settings**.

2. Touch **Security and Location**.

3. Touch **Set Unlock Pattern**. You're taken to a screen that gives directions for setting the pattern. Read them and then touch **Next**.

4. Read the next directions that appear, along with a brief display that illustrates how to draw the pattern. Touch **Next**.

5. On the next screen, draw your pattern. When you're satisfied with it, touch **Continue**.

6. You must confirm your pattern on the next screen by redrawing it. When you're satisfied with the pattern, touch **Confirm**.

7. You're returned to the **Security and Location** screen, but now notice that the **Require Pattern** and **Use Visible Pattern** options are selected. If you want to use these settings, you're done. You now must enter your set pattern before the phone is activated.

Now anyone who picks up your phone cannot access it unless you provide the lock pattern. If you think the lock pattern you've selected has ever been compromised, you can go back through those steps to reset it.

To turn off the lock pattern, go back to the **Security and Location** screen and deselect the **Require Pattern** option.

Yellow Box

When the lock pattern is enabled on your phone, you can still make emergency calls without unlocking the phone. All other functions are disabled until the correct lock pattern is entered.

Android 1.5 also has an additional security feature that didn't exist in the previous version of Android: the ability to set up a SIM card lock. This allows you to lock your SIM card so that anyone who picks up your phone will need a PIN number to access it.

To set the SIM card lock, go to **Menu > Settings > Security & Location** and select **Set up SIM card lock**. On the next screen, select **Lock SIM Card**. A Lock SIM card dialog box appears. Type in the pin that you want to use and touch **OK**. Now your SIM card is locked and you'll have to have the PIN to access it. You can also change the pin at any time by selecting the **Change SIM PIN** option. Just remember, once you set the PIN, if you forget it, you can't access your own phone.

Closing the Door

By now, you should be comfortable with the location of all the buttons on your phone and how to navigate the various touch-screen menus. You may also have chosen to pattern-lock or SIM lock your phone to keep others away from your personal information.

Next up, we run through some of the basic operations of the phone: managing calls, messages, and the like. In Chapter 3, we also cover some of the essentials of syncing your phone with online services and your computer.

Basic Use of Your Android Phone

M ost mobile phones are fairly simple to use. The Android phones are not much different from other touch-screen phones, either, so they're fairly intuitive. This chapter is a quick run-through of basic communicating using the Android phone. If you're already pretty familiar with your Android phone, you can skim this chapter. Don't skip it entirely—you might find a few tips and tricks that you didn't know about.

Phone Calls

Making phone calls with the Android phone is simple and works much like making calls with any other mobile phone. However, you can make calls in numerous ways, which means you can choose the one that's easiest for you.

Your in-call, pre-call, and post-call capabilities might also be different. Some of the capabilities missing in the first Android release were corrected when Android 1.5 was released, however. For all others, there are some third-party applications that can help with missing functionality.

Calling Methods

Your first phone call could be just a couple taps away. You can make calls in six different ways, depending on what you're doing at any given time.

No **Joke**   Making calls with the Android phone might be easy, but you'll get nowhere if your phone goes into sleep mode. If that's the case, press any button and then press the **Menu** button (or press the Menu button twice) to wake up the phone. You can also bring your phone out of sleep mode by sliding open the keyboard.

■ **Call button**—The Call button works like that of most phones. A short press on the Call button (when the phone isn't in sleep mode) brings up your call log, shown in Figure 3.1. From there, you can select any number in the log to call, or you can switch between tabs and use the dialer, your contacts, or your favorites. Two short presses on the Call button redials the last number you called.

■ **Onscreen Dialer**—The onscreen dialer is a number pad that appears on the screen of your phone when you select **Dialer** from your home screen or when you select the **Dialer** tab in the Call log. If the keyboard is open, the onscreen dialer does not appear. Instead, you'll see a message to dial using the keyboard.

■ **Contacts**—You can dial calls directly from your contact listings. Select **Contacts** from the home screen or from the call log, and then select the name of the contact you want to call. You can scroll through your contacts using the fast-scroll capability by dragging your finger quickly from the top of the screen toward the bottom. You'll also notice a small gray button that appears on the right side of the screen when you're scrolling. If you touch and hold this button as you scroll, each letter of the alphabet is displayed as you scroll. When you find the correct contact, touch the contact name to select it; then touch the number you want to dial.

FIGURE 3.1

The Call Log lists all the calls you've made, received, and missed. The available storage space on your phone determines the number of calls shown on the list.

■ **MyFaves**—MyFaves is a feature that's specific to T-Mobile. Using the MyFaves option, you can dial anyone who is listed as one of your MyFaves contacts. To place a call to one of those contacts, touch the **MyFaves** icon and then touch the icon for one of your favorite contacts, as shown in Figure 3.2. This brings you to a menu of contact options, where you can initiate a call by selecting **Call**. If you're using a phone that has been unlocked and is in use on another network, the MyFaves icon won't show on your phone.

■ **Voice Dialer**—The Voice Dialer feature of the phone isn't immediately visible. No icon for it automatically appears on the home screen, but you can find the icon in the applications menu. You can also access the Voice Dialer by pressing and holding the green call button until the Voice Dialer appears. Then just say "Call" and the name you want to call. Speak clearly and loudly enough for the phone to pick up your voice. After the voice dialer translates your voice command, it confirms the person that you want to call. Touch **OK** to initiate the call. If the name of the person that appears is incorrect, touch **Cancel**.

■ **Click to Dial**—You can dial a phone number from a website or document. When you're in a document or on a website that contains a phone number, highlight the number using your finger or using the scrollbar, and then click it. The dialer appears, with the number entered; you can either touch the green button on the right side of the number or press the green call button on the bottom of the phone.

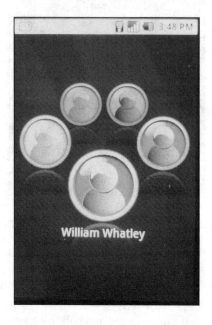

FIGURE 3.2

Touch one of the MyFaves icons to begin a call to that person.

One more call option exists: When you're connected to a Wi-Fi network, you can use a *voice over IP (VoIP)* connection. VoIP enables you to use the Internet to make phone calls instead of placing them through your wireless provider.

Voice over IP (VoIP) is a method of voice data delivery that uses the Internet to transfer packets of voice data from one location to another. Traditional landline phones use specialized voice data lines to transfer the same data. In comparison, VoIP uses the Internet and specialized software to transfer voice data, but the end result is the same: a telephone call.

You won't find this capability preinstalled on your phone however. The application that enables VoIP calls wasn't released until after the phone hit the market. iSkoot for Skype is a VoIP application that works on both a Wi-Fi network and your wireless carrier's network. In a matter of minutes you can download it for free from the Android Market.

After installing iSkoot, you can use it either on the carrier's network that you're subscribed to (such as T-Mobile or AT&T) or on a Wi-Fi network. When using iSkoot on the carrier's network, normal voice and data charges still apply, but you'll be able to talk to other Skype users. When you're using it on the Wi-Fi network, only data charges apply; if you're subscribed to an unlimited data plan, you should incur no additional charges.

If you plan to use iSkoot, you need to have a Skype account. iSkoot works only with other Skype users; you can't use it to call just anyone. Creating a Skype account through the application is easy, though. After it's installed, select **Create Account** (see Figure 3.3), choose a username and password, and then wait while the account is created and synchronized. Then you can begin adding friends to your Skype account.

FIGURE 3.3

Each time you start the iSkoot for Skype application, you must either sign in with an existing account or create a new account.

You can also get a Skype account through the Skype website at www.skype.com and then use that account to sign in through iSkoot. Downloading Skype for your PC and creating a Skype account are both free, as is using Skype to contact other Skype users.

If VoIP interests you, check out the iSkoot for Skype application. It's another way to make calls using your Android phone—and a great way to have your Skype with you wherever you roam.

Call Capabilities

The G1 also offers other capabilities similar to those you'll find in other cellphones or even landline phones, such as call forwarding and call waiting. Consider this list of what's available on the G1:

- **Call Log**—The call log (refer to Figure 3.1) is useful for more than just placing calls. A quick glance at your call log not only tells you who you've called (indicated by a green arrow), who has called you (indicated by a blue arrow), and what calls you've missed (indicated by a red arrow), but it also tells you the duration of the call and an estimate of how long it's been since the call took place. One thing many people don't like about the call log is the estimate of how long it's been since the call took place. Many users would prefer to see an exact time and date of the call. As part of the update to Android 1.5, a new feature added is the ability to see detailed information about your call. Just touch any listing in the call log to bring up an information screen where you'll see details about when the call took place and how long it lasted. There's also information there to allow you to call that person again, send an SMS message, and view their contact listing.

- **MyFaves activity log**—The MyFaves activity log is much like the call log, except that it's specific to your MyFaves contacts. To access the log, select the **MyFaves** icon and then select one of your MyFaves contacts. In the menu that appears, select **Activity Log** to see a list of dates on which calls were made to or received from that contact, as shown in Figure 3.4. Touch any instance on the activity log to call that person. But don't expect any more information about those calls; the only information the activity log lists is whether the call was incoming or outgoing and the date on which the call took place. Note that the MyFaves activity log is limited only to phones that are on the T-Mobile network. Phones on other wireless carrier networks won't have this option.

FIGURE 3.4

The MyFaves activity log shows incoming and outgoing calls to specific members of your MyFaves list.

■ **Call Forwarding**—If you can't be available to answer incoming calls, you can choose to have them forwarded to another number. By default, your calls are set to forward to your voice mail number, but you can change that by going to **Settings > Call Settings** and touching **Call Forwarding**. On the Call Forwarding Settings page, you can change when you want calls to be forwarded and to what number you want to forward them by touching one of the options. If you want to have your calls forwarded to different numbers when yours is busy, when a call is unanswered, or when you're unreachable—like when you're out of signal range—you can do so.

■ **Call Waiting**—Call waiting allows a call to ring through even when you're already on a call. You can disable call waiting by going to **Settings > Call Settings > Additional Call Settings** and deselecting call waiting by touching the box with the green check mark. You can enable call waiting again by touching that same box when it's empty, to place a green arrow in it.

3

■ **Caller ID**—On the same **Additional Call Settings** screen as the Call Waiting option is the Caller ID option. With this option, you let your network determine whether your number should be displayed on outgoing calls, whether you want to hide your number all the time, or whether you want to show your number all the time.

■ **Swap Calls**—You can switch between two calls while on a call. To swap calls, press the **Menu** button while on the call; then from the menu that appears, touch the **Swap Calls** option.

■ **Add Call**—When you're already having one conversation, you can create a group conversation by using the Add Call option. During a call, press the **Menu** button and then choose **Add Call**. The onscreen Dialer appears, and you can use the tabs above it to navigate to the call log or your contacts. Just place the call as usual; once connected, you can merge the two calls for a group conversation.

■ **Hold**—You can place a call on hold if you have another call coming in or you want someone to wait while you do another quick task. You can place a call on hold in two ways. First, simply press the Call button when the second call comes through. Second, press the **Menu** button and select **Hold**. To return to the previous call, hang up the current call or use the **Swap Calls** option.

■ **Mute**—If you have something you want to say but you don't want the person on the other end of the line to hear it, you can use the Mute option. To access the Mute option, press the **Menu** button and then touch **Mute**. You can unmute the call by pressing the Mute option again.

■ **Speaker**—Your Android phone also has a speaker capability, which enables you to use the phone like a speaker phone. Just press the **Menu** button while on a call and touch the **Speaker** option. Use the same actions to turn off the speaker phone.

■ **Bluetooth**—If you have a Bluetooth headset, you can use it with your Android phone. First, you must pair the headset with the phone, using the pairing instructions for the headset (make sure Bluetooth is enabled on your phone). Then you can connect to your headset while you're on a call by pressing the **Menu** button and then touching **Bluetooth**.

Yellow Box

On some phones, you can use Bluetooth to transfer files such as pictures or ring-tones between phones. That's not the case with the Android phone. Straight out of the box, the Android phone's Bluetooth capabilities are available only for use with a Bluetooth headset. At the time this book was written, no third-party applications extended Bluetooth capabilities to file transfers. Don't be discouraged, though. Search the Android Market, because new applications become available every day.

In addition, you can use your phone locally or abroad (if your service contract allows), and you can access the other features of your phone while on a call by pressing the back arrow after the call has initiated until you're back to the home screen.

No Joke

If you're planning to take your Android phone abroad, check into your calling plan. Many people don't realize that the Android phone draws on the technology used to transfer data and access the Internet, even for phone calls. That means when you go abroad, even if you have turned off all data capabilities, your phone will still use data capabilities, at roaming rates. You'll come home from your trip abroad with more than just memories—you could also face a hefty cellphone bill.

Text Messages, Multimedia Messages, and IMs

Phone calls are great, but these days, people stay connected in many other ways. Text messages, multimedia messages, and IMs are also part of the communication arsenal—and for some, life ceases to exist without these capabilities. The Android phone offers rich messaging applications, so it should appeal to those who prefer to use messaging in place of conversation.

A full keyboard enhances the messaging capabilities of the G1, but that's not the only enhancement you'll find. For example, sending multimedia messages is easy, and you're not limited to sending your multimedia files through text messaging; you can also send them through email and upload them to some social media services. The myTouch doesn't have a slide-out keyboard like the G1, but the onscreen keyboard is responsive and easy to use, with all the same capabilities of the slide-out keyboard. A plus, too, is that you can change settings to make it more tactile with vibration and sound on a key touch.

Text Messages

Text messaging with the Android phone is simple. To send a text message, just touch the **Messaging** icon on the home screen. You'll see a list of existing text message strings, shown in Figure 3.5 (if there are any). If you have not yet sent or received text messages, the only option you'll see onscreen is the **New Message** option.

FIGURE 3.5

The Messaging screen lists incoming and outgoing text messages in date order.

Touch the **New Message** option to start a new text message. Then enter the number to send the message to and enter your text into the body of the message. You must use the keyboard to enter this information. However, on the **To** line, you can begin typing the name of the person you want to send the message to; a list of possible matches appears below the line. As you type more letters in the name, the list of available options narrows. When you see the person you want to send the message to, touch the correct name to add it to the **To** line.

When you've composed your text message, touch the **Send** option. The message moves to the center of the screen, and a small red envelope appears beside it until sending is complete. After the message has been sent, a green envelope icon appears briefly to let you know the send was successful. If you see a yellow caution icon, a problem occurred while sending the message. You'll also receive notification in the status bar if the message doesn't send properly.

Incoming message notifications are displayed in the status bar. When you receive a message, pull down the *window shade* and touch the message notification to go to the messaging window to view and reply to the message.

geek speak   The window shade is another name for the status bar. It's called a window shade because you can pull it down or push it up, just as you would a window shade.

Text messaging is pretty intuitive on the Android phone—and because it is the Android phone, you have many more options than just sending plain text messages. You can also take advantage of multimedia messages, instant messages, and even email.

Multimedia Messages

Multimedia messages include pictures or audio attachments. With the Android phone, sending a multimedia message starts either through the text message interface or directly from the file you want to send.

To start in the text message interface, follow these steps:

1. From the **Home** screen or the applications menu, touch **Messaging**.

2. Choose a person to send the message to from your existing message threads, or touch **New Message** to start a new thread.

3. Enter the recipient information and the text that you want to send in the message. Then press the **Menu** button.

4. Select **Attach** from the menu options. Another pop-out menu appears, as shown in Figure 3.6.

5. Select the type of media you want to attach from the available formats: Pictures, Camera, Video Audio, Record Audio, Slideshow. An appropriate menu for the chosen selection appears. Table 3.1 details the options you have for each media type.

6. Follow the onscreen prompts to attach the file. Then touch the **Send** option. The message sends just like a text message, showing the same sent or not sent icons you would see with a plain text message, and appears in your text message threads.

FIGURE 3.6

Use the Attach menu to choose the multimedia files to add to your text messages.

Table 3.1	Multimedia File Type Options
Pictures	The Pictures option takes you to your pictures file. Select the picture you want to attach. You return to the multimedia message to finish composing and sending it.
Capture Picture	This option opens the camera for you, to take a picture to send. Take the picture and then touch **Select This Picture** to send it, or, if you're not happy with the photo, touch **Capture New Picture** to take it again.
Audio	This opens your audio file. Select the file you want to attach and touch **OK** to return to the message-composing screen. Note that you cannot send songs that you have stored in the Music application from this option.
Video	This option allows you to attach existing videos to a message. When you touch **Video**, it takes you to the Select Video screen where you choose the video you want to send.
Capture Video	When you select this option the video function of your Android phone activates. Record the video you want to send (You'll learn more about recording videos in Chapter 4), and once the recording is finished choose **Play** to preview the video, **Attach** to add it to the message, or **Cancel** to start over from the beginning.
Record audio	This option opens the audio recorder so that you can record your voice or other sounds to send in the message. On the screen that appears, press the circle to begin recording and the square to end the recording. A timer displays the length of the recording. After you've stopped the recording, touch **Use This Recording** to attach it to the message or touch **Discard** to start again.

Slideshow	The Slideshow option enables you to create a photo slideshow to send as a multimedia message. Select **Slideshow** to go to a screen where you can use existing slides or add new ones. When you add a new slide, you can choose a picture to add to that slide. If the picture size is too large for the slideshow, you're asked if you want it automatically resized. Touch **Yes** to process the photo. When you're happy with your slideshow, finish populating the message and touch **Send**.

Sending a multimedia file directly from the file you want to send is easy, too. Navigate to the file you want to send, press the **Menu** key, and select **Share**. A **Share Picture Via** menu appears, as shown in Figure 3.7. You should see options to share via Google Mail and Messaging, but if you have third-party applications (such as MySpace and Picasa) installed, you might also have options for sharing via those services. Chapter 9, "Adding Applications to Your Device," covers adding third-party applications to your device, if you want to learn more about those options.

FIGURE 3.7

The Share Picture Via menu gives you options for the different ways you can send media files to other people, including core applications and third-party apps.

Select **Messaging** to send a multimedia text message. Then you'll see the blank message. Add a recipient, insert any text you want to include, and press **Send**. As with a regular text message, you should see sending status and notification icons.

One more note about messaging with the Android phone. It can save your messages as a draft. If you're in the midst of creating a message and the phone rings, a draft is automatically saved to the device. When you're ready to finish the message, just go to that message thread and you'll see the **Draft** notation, in red beside the message. Just tap it to continue editing the message.

With the capabilities of the Android phone, you can add files and create messages in convenient ways for whatever task you're performing at the time. You're also not limited to text messages and multimedia messages—the Android phone comes with instant messaging capabilities as well.

Instant Messages

Instant messages are much like text messages or multimedia messages, but they work with other people who are online, not necessarily just those for whom you have a phone number. The Android phone comes with several options for sending instant messages.

Because the Android phone is Android based and many of the core applications belong to Google, you automatically have the Google Talk IM service enabled on your phone. On the Android phone, Google Talk behaves similarly to text messaging. You receive Google Talk messages as if they were text messages, and they're archived with previous text messages.

Yellow Box Google Talk is Google's answer to instant messaging. It's an application that's both part of Gmail and standalone through the downloadable Google Talk app. It allows you to instant message other Google account users (which means they're also Gmail users, because you're signed up for Gmail when you sign up for a Google account).

The real difference is that, with Google Talk, other Google Talk users can message you on your phone. You don't have to be on a computer; you just need a connection through your phone. You do have to initialize your Google Talk account on your Android phone before it becomes active, but after you do that, it's always on.

To activate the Google Talk account, select **IM** from the applications menu. The **Select Account** window appears, as shown in Figure 3.8. You should see options for AIM, Google Talk, Windows Live Messenger, and Yahoo! Messenger. Touch **Google Talk**; you're prompted to enter your Google Talk account username and password. Your Friends list then is displayed on your screen.

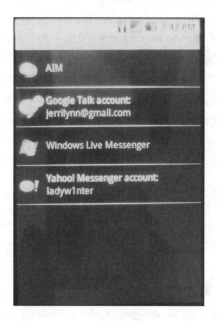

FIGURE 3.8

Use the Select an Account window to choose which IM service you want to connect to. You can use multiple services.

A green dot indicates friends who are online, and their picture appears next to their name (if they have set up a picture or avatar to display). Friends who are not online are shown with a gray circle that contains an X, and no picture is displayed.

Also on the screen is your status icon and the avatar or picture that is displayed by your name when you're using Google Talk with another person. You can change that picture by touching it and selecting a new one, and you can change your status by touching the small button next to your picture and selecting a new status.

Google Talk isn't the only option you have for instant messaging. As you saw, AIM, Windows Live Messenger, and Yahoo! Messenger are also available options.

To set up any one of those accounts, touch the account type in the **Select Account** screen. Then follow the onscreen prompts to sign in or create an account. All the accounts work in much the same way. Your status is displayed, although not all of the IM accounts allow for pictures or avatars. You also have a friends list that shows who is available or online and who is not.

In each IM account, you also have a set of available options that you can access by pressing the **Menu** button. The options differ a little with each program, depending on how the IM service is set up, but you'll see these basics:

- Capabilities to view, add, or remove contacts
- Capability to block users from contacting you
- Account list that takes you to the IM accounts page
- Settings options
- A sign-out option

One cool factor with the IM capabilities of the G1 is that you can be signed into multiple IM applications at any given time. So if you're using both Google Talk and Yahoo! Messenger, or even if you're using all the available IM applications, you can have as many open at any given time as you like.

To Sync or Not to Sync

Now you know the basic ways in which you can communicate with your phone. The next part of the book covers more ways. Chapters 4–9 walk you through the various core applications that come preinstalled on the phone, and you'll see some of the third-party apps that can replace or enhance those core apps. But before we jump into that part of the book, we need to cover syncing up your data.

When you hear the term *sync* or *data sync*, you might think in terms of plugging your phone into your computer and allowing an application to automatically copy data from your device to your computer or from the computer to the device so that the two match. That's a common method of backing up and synchronizing data with many types of devices—just not with the G1.

Sync and *data sync* are terms that both refer to the same thing: transferring data from your device to your computer or from your computer to your device so there are mirror images of the data in both places. A data sync is a good way to create a backup copy of everything that's on your device; if something happens to your device, you can replace all the data with one simple action. A data sync is also useful for ensuring that you have access to all your contacts and data files on both the device and the computer.

The Android phone doesn't come with a sync application, and as this is written, no third-party data sync application is available. Now here's the confusing part: You can still sync your data to the computer or web applications. You just do this in a different way than you might think of with traditional sync methods.

Syncing with the Web, Not the Desktop

One way in which you can sync your data is with some of the core apps that come with the phone. These core apps—Gmail, Contacts, Calendar, and so on—are web based, so you're not technically syncing them with your computer; you're using the applications on the web.

You can set syncing to happen automatically, or you can run a sync only when you want to. Here's how to set it up:

1. From the **Home** screen, open the apps menu and select **Settings**.

2. On the Settings screen that appears, touch **Data Synchronization**.

3. This opens the Data Synchronization page, shown in Figure 3.9. To have your Gmail, Calendar, and Contacts information sync automatically, make sure there is a check mark in the **Auto-sync** box. (Touch the box to check or uncheck it.)

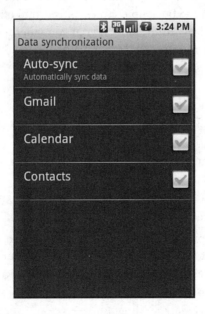

FIGURE 3.9

The Data synchronization page enables you to choose what you want to sync and when you want those syncs to happen.

4. Then you can select which of the applications to sync on the automatic schedule. Place or remove check marks next to the apps you want to sync. You can choose one, a combination, or all of the apps.

5. When you're finished, press the Back key to back out of the menu, leaving the settings in place. You won't find a "save settings" option on the menu; changes are saved automatically when you return to a previous screen.

If you don't want an automatic sync to take place, you can sync apps only when you want to. Go to the same **Data Synchronization** screen, select the apps you want to sync, and then press the **Menu** key. A **Sync Now** option appears at the bottom of the screen, as shown in Figure 3.10. Touch that option to sync data.

Some third-party applications may also have syncing capabilities, but each application determines this differently. Still, if you want to copy other data on your phone over to your computer, or if you want to move data on your computer over to your phone, you can sync that in another way, too.

You Can Still Sync With the Desktop—Sorta

Not all the data on your phone is confined to Gmail, Calendar, or Contacts. You might want to back up pictures, music, and other data files. Or maybe you want to have certain files on your computer moved to your phone. You can sync those files by connecting the phone to your computer using the USB cable that came along with it.

When you connect your phone to your computer in this way, you must first *mount* the device as a drive; then you can transfer files between the device and the computer. To mount the device, follow these steps:

1. Plug the USB cord into the phone and into the computer. When your computer recognizes the device, a USB icon appears in the status bar of the phone.

2. Pull down the window shade and touch **USB Connected** in the **Notifications** area.

3. You're prompted to mount the drive. Touch **Mount**. The AutoPlay screen for the device should appear on your computer. If it does not, navigate to **My Computer** to find the device.

After the device is mounted, you can transfer files back and forth between the device and the computer at will using a simple drag and drop method. When you're finished, simply unplug the device, and the files you moved should be on the device or the phone (or both), depending on what you moved.

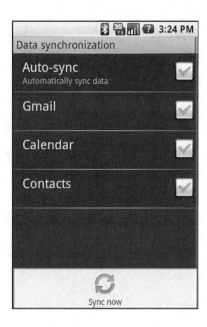

FIGURE 3.10
The Sync Now option appears when you press the Menu key while you're on the Data Synchronization screen.

Closing the Door

The basic use of your Android phone phone is pretty straightforward. Most screens on the phone are easy to navigate, and on most screens, the **Menu** button gives you additional options. You should find it easy to become familiar with making calls, sending messages, and even syncing your application data.

When you're familiar with these actions, you can really get into the fun parts of the phone: the applications. That's what we start covering in the next part of this book. Part II, "The Applications," is all about applications, and Chapter 4, "Core Applications," is your first in-depth look at an application. In Chapter 4, you'll get really familiar with the core applications. That means covering all the capabilities. Let's get to it.

The Applications

In this part:

- Core Applications
- Going Online
- Email Anywhere
- Getting Around with GPS and Google Maps
- Breaking Boredom with Entertainment Options
- Adding Applications to Your Device

Google Phones are a pretty cool phone, but let's be honest: It's not what Android is all about. The phone is a device that will change so quickly that it's hard to get up-to-speed on one phone before the next is available. Android is really about the applications.

This part of the book looks at those applications more closely. In Chapter 4, "Core Applications," you'll get the lowdown on how to use some of the basic applications installed on the phone.

In Chapter 5, "Going Online," you'll see how to get online and use the Internet for both fun and function. Chapter 6, "Email Anywhere," extends that with an explanation of how to use the available mobile email services, including an in-depth look at Gmail mobile. Chapter 7, "Getting Around with GPS and Google Maps," takes you through Google Maps and some of the new features that were released with the Android phone.

Chapters 8, "Breaking Boredom with Entertainment Options," and 9, "Adding Applications to Your Device," round out this part of the book. In Chapter 8, you'll learn about the available entertainment applications, including music, videos, and a few games thrown in. And in Chapter 9, we walk through how to add new applications to your Android phone using the Android Market.

The applications really are the meat of any Android-based phone, so you'll have a lot of fun with this section. You'll be amazed at what's out there and what you can do with it. So why wait any longer? Let's see the goodies.

Core Applications

The draw of an Android-based phone is that developers can do so many things with applications for the phone. As with the iPhone, the application possibilities are endless. Another draw is that users can build upon, access, or add to the set of core applications.

Those core applications help you accomplish basic things, such as stay in touch with people, stay on time, and capture the world around you. You'll probably use these core applications more than any others.

Connecting with Contacts

If you'll use your phone most to make calls and send messages, the Contacts application is probably the one you'll access the most. This application is designed to hold all the information you'll need for the people you communicate with. That includes multiple types of contact methods:

- Pictures
- Phone numbers
- Email addresses
- IM names
- Postal addresses
- Company names
- Notes about the contact

In addition to the contact information, you can set numbers to dial by default when you choose a contact, choose individual ringtones, and even send calls from a specific contact directly to voice mail. No more irritating solicitors: Just relegate them to voice mail land, and your phone won't even ring.

To get to your contacts, touch the **Contacts** icon on the **Home** screen of your phone. Alternatively, you can touch the onscreen **Menu** and select the **Contacts** icon.

As you saw in Chapter 3, "Basic Use of Your Android Phone," the Contacts application is tied in with the Dialer, the Call Log, and your Favorite contacts. They're all different tabs on a single application. That integration makes it easier for you to communicate with your Contacts, but it also makes it easier to add new Contacts based on messages or calls that you've received.

The Contacts screen, shown in Figure 4.1, lists all the contacts that you have stored in your phone. On this screen, you'll see the names of your contacts and the default phone number that you use for them. Scroll through the list by dragging your finger up the page, or you can touch the small gray scroll handle to quickly scroll through your list alphabetically. When you scroll, each letter of the alphabet is displayed onscreen and as you scroll through those letters those contacts whose names start with that letter appear.

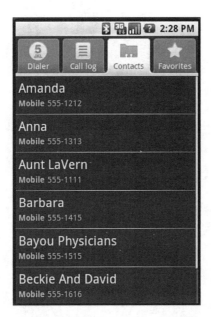

FIGURE 4.1

The Contacts screen lists all the contacts that you have stored on your phone. You can scroll through them to access contact information.

Adding Contacts

If you have a lot of Contacts, you'll appreciate the capability to scroll through them. The Android phones have SD memory card capabilities, so you can store all your contacts from Gmail on the phones. If you're like us, that's hundreds of people. And it seems like we're adding new contacts all the time. Fortunately, the Android phone gives you several options for adding contacts.

To add a new contact, follow these steps:

1. Touch the **Contacts** icon on the **Home** screen.

2. When your contacts appear, press the **Menu** key on the device. This opens a small menu at the bottom of the window.

3. Touch **New Contact**. This opens the contact form shown in Figure 4.2.

4. Enter the contact's name.

FIGURE 4.2

Fill in the New Contact form to create a new contact on your phone.

5. Enter the phone number. You can also touch the white number–type indicator to the left of the phone number to select a different type of phone:

> Home
>
> Mobile
>
> Work
>
> Work fax
>
> Home fax
>
> Pager
>
> Other
>
> Custom

6. Add an email address, if you want to include it. Again, you can use the type indicator box to the left of the email address to indicate the type of email address you want to add: Home, Work, Other, or Custom.

When you choose the Other option when designating a number or email address type, your only option is to have **Other** displayed as the type. However, you can select **Custom** to bring up a new window that enables you to type a custom label for that phone number or email address.

7. Choose a ringtone for the contact. If you want to use the same ringtone for all your calls, leave the **Default** option selected.

8. Select or deselect the option **Send Calls Directly to Voice Mail**. Just touch the checkbox to the right of the option to place a check mark in the box or to remove the check mark from the box.

9. Add + **More Info**. If you have contact information for this contact that you haven't found a field for, you can add it here. You can include such additional information as this:

    Phone—Additional Home, Mobile, Work, Work Fax, Home Fax, Pager, Other, and custom numbers

    Email—Additional Home, Work, Other, or Custom email addresses

    IM—Specific IM identities for AIM, Windows Live, Yahoo!, Skype, QQ, Google Talk, ICQ, and Jabber

    Postal address—Postal addresses for Home, Work, Other, and Custom

    Other—Additional information such as Organizational information and Notes

10. You can also remove any field in the contact file that has a red X to the right of the field. Just touch the **X** to remove the field.

11. When you've finished entering your contact's information, touch the **Save** option to save the contact. You then return to the main Contacts screen. If you change your mind about creating the contact, you can touch **Discard Changes** to have the form discarded and return to the main Contacts list.

Using the New Contact form isn't the only way to add contacts to your phone. You can also add a contact using these methods:

■ **From the Dialer**—Enter the number that you want to add to your contacts using the onscreen dialer, and then press the Menu key. Touch **Add to Contacts**, and then enter the contact information and save it.

- **From the Call log**—Long-touch a number on the Call log to open a menu of options available for that number. Touch **Add to Contacts**, and then enter and save the contact information.

- **From Messaging Capabilities**—When you're creating a text message or multimedia message, or even sending an IM, you can add the recipient of that message to your Contacts, too. Just long-touch the username, phone number, or email address. A menu appears. Select **Add to Contacts**, and then enter the contact information and save it.

- **From the Browser**—When you're browsing the Web, you can long-touch a phone number to bring up a menu of additional options (including Dial, Add Contact, and Copy). Touch **Add Contact**, and then enter and save the contact information.

You can also add a number to an existing contact by typing the number into the Dialer or long-pressing a number in your call log. Then press the **Menu** key and touch **Add to Contacts**. You then move to the contact list; select the name of the contact to which you'd like to add the number, and you move to the contact information screen. Make any necessary changes—such as changing the number type—and then touch **Save** to save the updated information and return to your contacts list.

Managing Existing Contacts

I grew up as the daughter of a career military man. Military families tend to move a lot. That means new phone numbers and addresses every time you turn around. The joke with our friends and family was always that they put our family in their address book in pencil because they knew it would change soon.

I find that my personal contacts are much the same. People move, change phone numbers, make career changes, and even get married all the time. Life is in constant change, so it's helpful to be able to implement any changes in just a couple of touches.

The easiest way to change a contact is to long-touch the contact name, either in the Call Log or in the Contact list. A menu appears similar to the one shown in Figure 4.3. Select **View Contact** from the menu to go to the contact information page. Press the **Menu** key to open a menu of options; select **Edit Contact**. Then just change or add the desired information and touch **Save**.

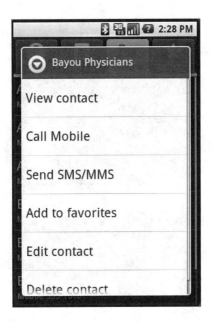

FIGURE 4.3

*Long-touch a contact to show a menu of available options for activities that you can perform
for that contact.*

You also might need to delete a contact. That's easy enough to do, too. In the
Contacts application, long-touch the contact you want to delete and touch
Delete Contact on the menu that appears. A confirmation message similar to
the one shown in Figure 4.4 appears. If you truly want to delete the contact,
touch **OK** and the contact will be deleted. You can also touch **Cancel** if you
change your mind, and the contact will remain intact.

 Use caution when deleting your contact information. Be sure that you truly want
to delete it before you touch **OK** in the confirmation message, because after you
delete the information, you can't retrieve it. If you inadvertently delete a contact,
you will need to re-create it from scratch.

You might like to know one last neat trick about your contacts. Unfortunately,
the Android phone doesn't have a speed-dial system set up. So each time you
need to call someone, you have to open the Dialer, the Call Log, or Contacts,
or (if you're a T-Mobile subscriber) use your MyFaves application. You can also
use the Voice Dialer, if that's your preference. But it can still be a little frustrating not to have speed-dial available.

FIGURE 4.4

Anytime you delete contact information, a confirmation message appears before the information is deleted.

One way to get around that frustration is to use a third-party application called AnyCut. AnyCut enables you to create shortcuts on your Home screen to any application or file on your device, even a phone number. So if you want a pseudo-speed-dial application, consider using AnyCut to create shortcuts to the people you call most often. Then all you have to do to initiate a call is touch the shortcut.

Saving the Date in the Calendar

Another frequently used core application is the Calendar. The calendar is a mobile version of Google Calendar and syncs with Google Calendar on the Web if you have a Google Calendar account. It's a good way to be sure you never forget an appointment: After you create an event on the calendar, you'll get reminders sent to your phone. If for some reason you're without your phone, you can access Google Calendar from the Web to find out what you have going on.

THERE'S MORE TO GOOGLE THAN MEETS THE EYE

Most people think of "Google, the search engine" when they think of Google, but there's so much more to Google than meets the eye. Google *is* a search engine, and when you go to www.google.com, you can search for documents, images, products, and much more. But Google also has a whole suite of productivity applications that the G1 enables you to take full advantage of.

For most of the productivity apps that are available through Google, you need only a single username and password. And they're all free. You can access productivity applications such as these with Google:

- Gmail
- Google Docs
- Google Spreadsheets
- Google Calendar
- Google Reader
- Picasa

In addition to these applications, YouTube is available for your G1. You can aggregate all these applications into a single page on the Web, iGoogle. To learn more about what applications are available and what you can do with those applications, go to www.google.com/intl/en/options/.

Navigating the Calendar

Using the Calendar feature on your phone is easy enough. To view the Calendar, just touch the **Calendar** icon. You might have to open the applications menu to find it because the Home screen does not automatically include a shortcut to the application.

When you touch the **Calendar** icon, you're automatically taken to your previous view of the calendar, whether it's Agenda, Day, Week, or Month view. You can change that view by pressing the **Menu** key. Then choose the display option you want to see.

You can also change the calendar view by picking a date on the Month view, or a day on the Week view. Long-press that date to open a menu that shows view options and enables you to add a new event. We return to the event-adding option in the next section ("Adding Events") of this chapter.

Yellow Box

Wouldn't it be nice if you could jump back to today's date when you're done jumping around any of the date views in the Calendar? You can. Just press the **Menu** button and then touch **Today** in the menu that appears. That brings you back to the current date in the same view.

In the Month view, days with appointments have a green indicator line to the right side of the date box, as shown in Figure 4.5. This line might show up at the top, at the bottom, in the middle, or broken into several places along the line. That indicates the rough time of day that the appointment appears on your calendar. If it's at the top, it's in the morning or all day. If it's at the bottom, that indicates afternoon or evening, and in the middle is (of course) the middle of the day. Broken lines indicate multiple appointments.

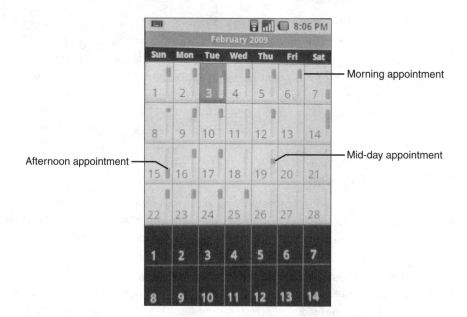

FIGURE 4.5

The Calendar Month view enables you to quickly see what days in a given month you have appointments scheduled and roughly when those appointments are scheduled.

You can switch between months by sweeping your finger up or down the screen. If you want a closer look at any given day in the month, just touch it to move to the Agenda view for that month. You can return to the month view when you're done by pressing the **Menu** key and touching **Month**.

In the Week view, shown in Figure 4.6, you're shown the current seven-day period (the week begins on Sunday and ends on Saturday). The current hour is highlighted in gray, and days that have an appointment are shown with a colored indicator in the hour of the appointment. If you have multiple, color-coded calendars set up, each appointment indicator will also have a colored dot on the left side, to indicate what calendar the appointment is stored on. If you don't have them yet but want to set up multiple calendars, keep reading. We show you how to set up additional calendars in the "Adding Multiple Calendars" section of this chapter.

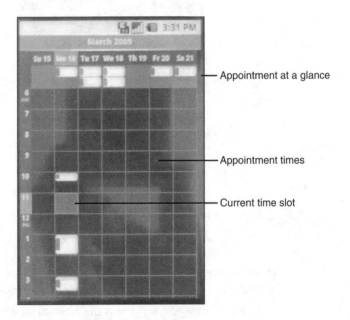

FIGURE 4.6

The Calendar Week view enables you to quickly see if you have appointments scheduled and what time they are scheduled for.

You can view past or future weeks by sweeping your finger to the left (past) or right (future) on the screen of the Android phone. If you want to quickly see what an appointment is without changing the view, just touch the event indicator. A small display box appears at the bottom of the screen to show brief details about the appointment (what it is and when it's scheduled).

The Day view shows you the contents of your calendar for a single day, as shown in Figure 4.7. Appointments appear at the top of the screen if they are all-day appointments, and on the appropriate time slot if they are shorter. The Day view is divided into one-hour increments. Appointments that take less than one hour show in shorter bars within the one-hour increments.

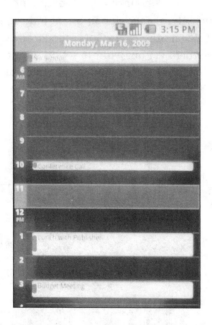

FIGURE 4.7

Appointments in the Day view show up within the one-hour increments preset within the view.

You can navigate from day to day in the same way that you navigate within the Week view—by sweeping your finger to the right or left on the screen.

One last view that you can use is the Agenda view, shown in Figure 4.8. Your capabilities are a little more limited in Agenda view. You can scroll through your Agenda view for the month by sweeping your finger up or down the screen. Touching an appointment takes you to a screen that displays only that appointment. Here you can see any Reminders set up for that appointment, or you can touch the **Menu** key from this screen and select **Add Reminder, Edit Event**, or **Delete Event**.

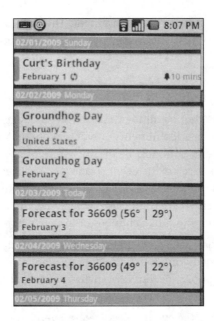

FIGURE 4.8
The Agenda view lets you see what appointments are on your schedule for a given day of the current month.

Adding Events

Adding events to the Calendar is pretty easy, but you must do it from within the application. To add an event—which Google calls an appointment—from any view, follow these steps:

1. Press the **Menu** button.

2. Touch **New Event**. The Event details screen appears.

3. Add the details of the event that you want to create. Details include what, when, where, description, calendar (if you have multiple calendars set up), reminders, and repeats.

4. When you're finished filling in the event creation form, touch **Save** to create the appointment. If you use Google Calendar online, this appointment will be copied to your calendar online the next time your calendar syncs.

You have other options for adding events, too. You can add events from any screen except the Agenda screen by using a long touch on the time or date that you want to add the appointment. Then follow the same steps to set the appointment. When you're done, you're returned to the previous view of the calendar.

Editing and Deleting Events

Appointments change all the time, so to be truly useful, you need a way to change or delete appointments on your calendar. You've got one. To delete or change an event, you must be in that event, or at least at a level that's far enough down to select the event specifically. That means that in the Month view, you have to select the day of the appointment that you want to change or delete. When you're at the level where you can select the appointment, follow these steps to make changes or to delete it:

1. From any screen where you can select the appointment to be changed or deleted, long-touch the appointment. This opens a menu of available options for that day, including the options Edit Event or Delete Event.

2. To delete the event, select **Delete Event**. A confirmation message appears to ensure that you actually want to delete the event. If you do, touch **OK**. If you change your mind, you can also touch **Cancel** to return to the previous screen.

3. To edit an event, touch the **Edit Event** option. This takes you to the same screen you saw when you created the event. Make whatever changes you need to make, and then touch **Save**. If you change your mind about the changes you're making, you can also select **Discard Changes** or you can delete the appointment completely by touching **Delete**.

When something changes, just change the event, or even delete it completely. Just be cautious—when you delete something, it's gone for good. The only way to replace it is to re-create it.

Adding Multiple Calendars

One last calendar capability that you might want to have access to is accessing multiple calendars that you've created with Google Calendar online. This is why you should use Google Calendar online. With multiple calendars, you can set up a different calendar (and color-code it) based on different areas of your life.

For example, if you have work appointments, sports schedules for multiple kids, and personal appointments that you want to keep up with, you can set up calendars for all of those and assign each calendar a color. Then when you create an appointment in that calendar, the event has the coordinated color attached so that you can tell at a glance whether an upcoming appointment is for you, for work, or for one of the kids.

Use these steps to add calendars to your calendar view on the G1:

1. From any screen within the Calendar application, press the **Menu** key.

2. Select **More** from the menu that appears.

3. Touch **My Calendars**. If you have other calendars that you've created on Google Calendar online, you should see them listed here. Otherwise, this screen is blank. Touch the small checkbox next to each calendar name to place a check mark next to the calendars that you want to add to the G1. Alternatively, you can touch that box to remove the check mark and remove them from the view.

4. Press the **Menu** key again to open a menu of available options.

5. Touch **Add Calendars**. A confirmation message appears; then touch **OK**.

6. The calendars are enabled on your G1. The next time the phone syncs with Google Calendar, the other calendars will be added to your calendar views.

Plenty of options are available in the Calendar application to help you make it your own. Of course, you might be a die-hard Outlook fan. And if you are, there's good news. A third-party application called Exchange By Touch will help you sync your Microsoft Outlook—including emails, calendar, and contacts—to your Android phone.

A third-party application called Background Calendar enables you to see your daily agenda as a background on your phone. You don't even have to open the Calendar application to see what's on your schedule for the day. No matter how you go about it, your Android-based phone has your dates covered.

Figuring with the Calculator

You can access your contacts and work with your calendar, but what about when you're out and need to figure a tip, balance your checkbook, or do some other mathematical calculation? If you're like us, you can do math in your head, but not quickly. Instead of carrying a calculator, now we just carry the G1 because it has the built-in Calculator application. And it's much easier to use than on other phones.

To access the Calculator, just open the applications menu and touch **Calculator**. As you can see in Figure 4.9, it's a pretty simple calculator. The onscreen keypad enables you to enter your calculations with a touch of your finger. If you need more advanced capabilities, you have access to those, too.

FIGURE 4.9

The calculator is basic and easy to use, but it has hidden advanced features if you need them.

To access the advanced features of the calculator, press the **Menu** key (from within the Calculator application) and then touch **Advanced Panel**. On the screen that appears, you'll find 12 advanced options, including square roots, parenthesis, and pi calculations. These options should be enough to get you through some intermediate calculations, but the calculator that's part of the core applications won't suffice for advanced math calculations.

Fortunately, third-party applications can help with that. If you need to have a tip calculator, several are available in the Android Market. But in addition to these tip calculators, you'll find Sci-Calc (a basic scientific calculator), ConvertAll (which enables you to convert between units of measurement), and

AgileMedCalc (a medical care–specific calculator). A dozen or so other calculators are also available that include everything from construction calculations to gaming calculations. And a quick search of the Android Market should turn up just about anything you need.

Using the Camera to Capture Pictures

You might remember the quick introduction to the camera in Chapter 2, "Getting to Know Android Phones." There you briefly learned how to activate the camera and take pictures. Remember, you can access the camera using the camera button on the right side of the unit, but only if you're on the Home screen. You have to press and hold the camera button until the camera activates.

You can access the camera another way if you're not in a hurry to get the camera open. Just open the applications menu and touch the **Camera** icon.

Taking pictures with the camera is a matter of pressing that same button on the right side of the device. Remember, however, that it's slow to take pictures, and if you're not careful, they'll be blurry. You can prefocus the camera, but sometimes it's more effective just to press the camera button and wait for the picture to focus and capture.

Camera Settings

You can't do much more with the camera than take pictures, but you need to know about a few controls. When the camera is active, you can press the **Menu** key to access two options: Pictures and Settings.

The Pictures option takes you to the pictures that you have taken and that are stored on your phone.

If you touch the **Settings** option, you move to the Camera settings page, shown in Figure 4.10. You can set two options on this page:

- **Store Location in Pictures**—This option enables you to add location data to your pictures when you save them. The information then appears in the details about the picture.

- **Prompt After Capture**—This option causes the device to prompt you to save after each picture that you take. If you want the camera to automatically save pictures to your device without being prompted, deselect the option.

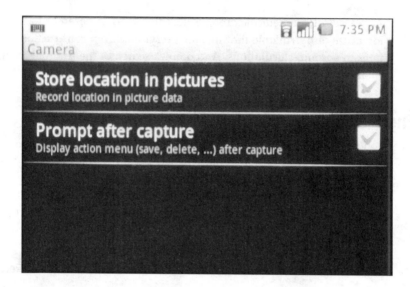

FIGURE 4.10

Use the Settings menu to set the location to store pictures and the prompts to receive after the capture.

Working with Pictures

Those are the only picture capabilities you have with your phone. However, when you're viewing your pictures, you have a few additional options. You can either view pictures directly from the Camera application by selecting **Pictures** from the menu options, or you can use the applications menu to get to your pictures by opening it and touching the **Pictures** icon.

How you enter the Pictures application determines what you see. If you enter from the Camera application, you see only the pictures that you've taken with the camera. If you enter through the apps menu, you see files for the Camera (pictures that you have taken), All Pictures, and Download (these are pictures you've downloaded from the Web).

If you enter from the apps menu, just touch the file that you want to open to view the pictures in that file. When you're in a file, you can also touch the individual pictures to view them separately from all the other files in that folder.

Let's step back for just a moment and look at the Pictures application. When you're viewing the available picture folders, you can press the **Menu** key to open options for the application. The options are Settings and Flip

Orientation. The Settings button takes you to the Camera application Settings screen, where you can work with different aspects of the pictures, including these:

- **Picture Size**—Choose whether to view individual pictures as large or small images.

- **Picture Sort**—Sort the way pictures are displayed in a folder, from newest to oldest or oldest to newest.

- **Confirm Deletions**—Check this option to ensure that you receive a confirmation message before you delete a picture. If you deselect the option, you won't receive a confirmation, so you could accidentally delete an image by touching the wrong button.

- **Slideshow Interval**—Set up how quickly pictures move when a slideshow has been activated. Choose from 2-, 3-, or 4-second intervals.

- **Slideshow Transition**—Select the transition options you want to see as the slideshow moves from one picture to another. You can choose Fade In & Out, Slide Left–Right, Slide Up–Down, or Random Selection.

- **Repeat Slideshow**—Select this option if you want a photo slideshow to run through all the pictures in the show more than one time.

- **Shuffle Slides**—This option enables you to show slides in random order when selected. Deselect to show pictures in the slideshow in the order in which they are stored in your picture folders.

The Flip Orientation option changes the orientation of the Pictures application. Touch the option to switch between landscape and portrait viewing modes.

Going a level deeper opens some new options for you. When you touch one of the picture folders, it opens to show you thumbnails of all the pictures inside that folder. When inside the folder view, press the **Menu** key to open another menu. This time, you have three options: Slideshow, Flip Orientation, and Settings.

You should be familiar with the Flip Orientation option, so let's look at the other two. The Slideshow option starts a slideshow for that folder. All the pictures in that folder immediately begin to play in slideshow mode when you touch the **Slideshow** option.

While the slideshow is active, you can touch the screen to pause the slideshow and show a set of available actions. Arrows to the right and left of the screen enable you to move through all the pictures in the file. The magnifying glasses at the bottom of the screen with + and – icons enable you to zoom in or out on a picture.

When you pause the slideshow, you must press the **Menu** key and touch **Slideshow** to begin the slideshow from its current location again. Other options in that menu include the following:

- **Share**—Touch this icon to open sharing options that enable you to send the picture you're viewing to others by Gmail, Messaging, MySpace, or Picasa, if you have them installed.

- **Rotate**—Choose Rotate to open a menu that enables you to rotate the displayed picture either right or left.

- **Flip Orientation**—Use this to change the orientation of the application from landscape to portrait.

- **Delete**—Choose this icon to delete the current picture from the slideshow and from the Pictures folder. You'll receive a confirmation before the delete action is complete, but after a picture is deleted, you can't get it back.

- **More**—Use this icon to access another menu that gives you these options: Crop (to crop a portion of a picture out of the background), Set As (to set the picture as a contact icon or wallpaper), Details (to show details about when and where the picture was taken), and Settings (to return to the Camera application settings page).

These options are the same options that you would see if you touched a specific picture to view instead of running the pictures in slideshow mode. The Camera application has no additional options, but you'll find some third-party applications that make pictures more useful and fun.

Picasa, a Google application, is one of those third-party applications. The Picasa app enables you to access pictures that you have stored in Picasa web albums, upload pictures to your Picasa account, or download them from your Picasa account to your device.

Another third-party application that you might find useful is SnapPhoto. This application uses the accelerometer that's already on your phone to add stability to your photos. Continuous Shoot is another third-party application that enables you to snap continuous pictures as long as you hold down the camera button.

Finally, Pictoral, a Picasa manager, is more functional than the Picasa third-party application that's available through Android Market. Pictoral makes managing your Picasa pictures from your device a little easier.

Capturing and Sharing Videos

One of the coolest features added when Android was updated to version 1.5 was video capability. Before the update, you were limited (on the T-Mobile G1) to viewing videos on YouTube. There was no method or capability for capturing video on your phone. But that all changed, and now you not only can capture and view video on your phone, but you can also share videos with other people using multi-media messaging and email. Yay, Android!

Capturing Video

Capturing video is a pretty straightforward task on the Android phone. From the menu, simply choose **Camcorder**. Remember, you can also put the Camcorder icon on the Home screen so that you don't have to dig into the menu to find it.

Once you touch the Camcorder icon, the video recording software that was added to Android 1.5 automatically boots up. You'll see a small film icon in the upper right corner (if you're viewing your screen in landscape; if you're viewing it in portrait mode, then the button is in the lower right corner). Touch this button to begin recording.

While you're recording, the film icon changes to a white button with a red dot in the center of it and a timer on the left side. This just indicates that you're recording and how long you have been recording. When you want to stop the video, simply press the button again to stop it.

Another thing you'll notice on your video screen is the small square on the left corner of the screen (again, that's if you're in landscape mode; if you're in portrait mode, it will be in the upper right corner). This is simply a preview of the previous video that you took. When you're recording, it disappears, and reappears when you stop recording.

If you want to preview your video when you're done recording, touch the preview window to open the last video you completed. This automatically switches to that video and four options appear: **Gallery** (which takes you to the video gallery), **Play** (plays the video), **Share** (allows you to share the video using MMS, YouTube or email), and **Delete** (deletes the video from your phone).

Press the Menu button while you're in the video recorder to open another menu that gives you three options: Switch to camera, Gallery, or Settings. The first two options are pretty self explanatory, but the Settings option allows you to change whether you want to have the location the video is taken along with the video and it allows you to select the video quality. You'll want to use the high quality setting if you just plan to take the videos and store them on your phone, or the low video quality when you want to send the video via some form of messaging.

Sharing Videos

Sharing your videos really isn't much different from sharing your pictures. Once you've recorded a video that you want to share, choose the share option from the options that are displayed on the preview screen.

You're prompted to choose between email, messaging, and YouTube. Select the method you want to use to share the video and then complete the process using the prompts on the screen. Easy, right?

It really is. And to finally have the ability to share videos is a major plus for the Android platform. The lack of video capability was one of the most glaring exceptions to the first version of Android. It's nice that the good folks in charge listened when people complained.

Closing the Door

The core applications that are included on the G1 are a good basis on which much can be built. Contacts, Calendar, Calculator, and Camera are all useful applications that enable you to stay in touch, stay on time, keep numbers straight, and capture important memories while you're out and about. But the phone also contains more core applications.

Several more that you can explore include the browser, Gmail, Google Maps, and entertainment applications, but those are all pretty involved applications that require more space to cover. Each one gets its own chapter, starting with the browser, which we cover in Chapter 5, "Going Online." Keep reading to learn how to get online and make the most of your browsing experience.

Going Online

The first thing users want to do when they get an Internet-enabled cellphone is to go online. That's doubly true if you have a touch phone because the screen is bigger, which means you have more capabilities. The Android phone is no exception. It is a little different, though.

Google backs Android, so the whole operating platform is designed with web functionality in mind. That's part of what makes an Android-based phone so special. Other phones enable you to connect to the Internet, but they don't enable you to interact with it. Android does. And it all starts with the web browser and getting online.

Getting Connected

Before we get too deep into connecting to the Internet, we need to take a detour. Don't worry, we'll get back on the right track. But it's important that you know how connected you can be with the Android phone: All that connectedness can work together to give you a richer Internet experience.

Connection Is More Than Just the Internet

Most of this chapter is about connecting to the Internet and using the web browser, but you can connect in more ways with the Android phone. In addition to your wireless carrier's connection, you can connect to other services, such as these:

- **Wi-Fi**—This is a wireless network similar to what you might have in your home or that you'll find in various places such as coffee shops and restaurants. It enables you to connect to the Internet through a router. These networks might not be secure, so you should understand the risks of connecting to them.

- **Bluetooth**—A Bluetooth connection won't help you get connected to the Internet. In fact, the only thing you can currently use Bluetooth for on the Android phone is to connect to a Bluetooth device for hands-free calling. However, future iterations of Android (and the Android phone) should include Bluetooth capabilities for exchanging files and for connecting to other Bluetooth devices such as audio equipment or printers.

- **Global Positioning System (GPS)**—This is a satellite connection that enables location services such as mapping and even device tracking. This is important because many third-party applications work with both the Internet and the GPS capabilities of the Android phone to enable social networking and other services.

Including the wireless carrier's connection, you have four methods of connecting to services on the Android-based phone. Two of those methods—the wireless carrier's network and the Wi-Fi connection—enable you to connect to the Internet. You're required to have a data plan with the Android phone because the wireless carrier connects to the Internet for everything that it does: calls, syncing, and even text messaging.

Although calls are not routed through the Internet unless you're using a Skype service, the Android phone connects to it as calls are incoming or outgoing. Syncing needs to take place over the Internet because, as you learned in Chapter 4, "Core Applications," most of the Android phone's core applications are actually web-based versions of Google applications. You can use web-based versions of third-party applications to enhance the other applications.

Text messaging is a form of data transfer all wireless carriers use; a data connection instead of a voice connection. That's why all wireless carriers have separate voice and data plans. It's no different on the Android phone. Your text and multimedia messages travel across a data connection that, in essence, is an Internet connection.

A Bit More on Bluetooth and GPS

The other two connections—Bluetooth and GPS—are used for services such as mapping, tracking, and audio connections. These are standalone services, but developers can also connect them to other applications for use in web-based programs.

However, these two services can seriously drain the Android phone's battery life. Both Bluetooth and GPS have *radio* capabilities. That means they're always on and they're always eating battery life, as if it's fine chocolate.

geek speak

Radio in an application means that the application sends out a search signal periodically. For example, a GPS radio periodically sends out a GPS signal, trying to locate a GPS network to which it can connect. If no such network is found, the application resends the search signal after a specified amount of time. If a compatible network is found, the application tries to connect to that network. When connected, it remains connected until the network is out of range or is manually disconnected.

To help preserve your battery life, you need to know how to enable the Bluetooth and GPS when you need it and disable it when you don't.

Follow these steps to enable or disable Bluetooth:

1. From the **Home** screen, press the **Menu** key and select **Settings**. Alternatively, from the **Home** screen, touch the applications menu, and then select **Settings**.

2. The Settings screen opens. Touch **Wireless Controls**.

3. The Wireless controls screen opens, as shown in Figure 5.1. To enable Bluetooth, touch the checkbox to the right of **Bluetooth** to place a check mark in it. To disable it, touch the box again to remove the check mark.

4. When you're finished, press the **Home** key to save your settings and return to the Home screen.

FIGURE 5.1

You manage your Bluetooth connectivity and settings from the Wireless Controls screen.

Just because you have Bluetooth enabled doesn't mean that you're connected to another device. To connect the Android phone with a wireless device, you need to go into the Bluetooth Settings menu. When you touch **Bluetooth Settings**, it opens the Bluetooth Settings menu, shown in Figure 5.2. If you want your device to be *discoverable* by other devices, touch the checkbox to the right of **Discoverable** to enable that feature. To turn off discoverability, touch the box again. If you want to have other devices connected to the Android phone, the Discoverable option must be selected.

The Bluetooth settings page also shows your device name and a list of the Bluetooth devices that you have paired with. If you no longer want to connect with a device on that list, long-touch the device name, and then select **Unpair**. This removes the pairing relationship. You can also long-touch a device name to connect to it.

To pair the Android phone with another Bluetooth device, make sure it's discoverable, and then put the other device in pairing mode. That device should recognize the Android phone; then you're prompted on the Android phone to create the pairing. Select the Pairing option and enter the security code (if one exists); the pairing then is complete. After you've paired a device with the Android phone, they will pair up automatically each time the device is operational and the Android phone is discoverable.

FIGURE 5.2

Use the Bluetooth Settings menu to turn Bluetooth on, to make it discoverable, or to see what devices you have a pairing relationship with.

Yellow
Box

Remember that currently you can use the Android phone only with Bluetooth headsets, not with other Bluetooth devices. Although you might be able to pair the Android phone with other devices, attempting to transfer files between them will result in an error. Hopefully, Bluetooth applications that support additional Bluetooth capabilities will be added to the Android Market in the future.

5

Enabling and disabling the GPS system works the same way; however, those controls are located in a slightly different spot. Chapter 7, "Getting Around with GPS and Google Maps," further explains the device's GPS capabilities and associated applications. For now, these steps will help you enable or disable your GPS capabilities:

1. From the **Home** screen, press the **Menu** key and select **Settings**. Alternatively, from the **Home** screen, touch the **Applications** menu and then select **Settings**.

2. The Settings screen opens. Touch **Security and Location**.

3. The **My Location Sources** screen, shown in Figure 5.3, opens. To enable GPS, touch the checkbox to the right of **Enable GPS Satellites** to place a check mark in it. To disable it, touch the box again to remove the check mark.

FIGURE 5.3

My Location Sources enables you to select whether you want to use the GPS capabilities, in addition to other options.

4. When you're finished, press the **Home** key to save your settings and return to the Home screen.

A third-party application makes it easier to enable or disable GPS, Bluetooth, and a handful of other capabilities. The application, called Toggle Settings, enables you to toggle on and off the different networking services and some of the different settings on your phone (such as brightness and vibrate). If you place a shortcut to the application on your Home screen, you can turn services on or off with two touches, in most cases. You can find Toggle Settings in the Android Market.

Yellow Box

Adding a shortcut to your Home screen is easy. Just open the applications menu and long-touch the application for which you want to add a shortcut. When you feel the device vibrate briefly, drag the icon to the Home screen. If you want to remove the icon, long-touch it again until the device vibrates, drag it to the application menu launcher (which changes to look like a trash can), and release it. The shortcut is removed from your Home screen.

The Important Stuff: Wi-Fi

Connecting through the GPS or Bluetooth applications is cool. It enables you to access some more useful features on the phone. But the real fun comes when you connect to Wi-Fi. Wi-Fi enables you to connect to the Internet through an existing wireless network, without being charged for the data transfer.

This is important. If you're using a limited data plan and you use more than your allotted amount of data transfer (and data transfers every time you connect to the Web, load a web page, download a file, or do anything while you're online), you could wind up with a shocking wireless bill. Avoid the heart attack.

UNDERSTANDING WIRELESS DATA PLANS

Wireless data plans can be confusing. Sometimes you think you're getting unlimited connection capabilities, but then when your bill comes in, you find out that your idea of connection and your wireless company's idea of connection are two different things. That's why it's always best to understand how you use your phone before you purchase a data plan. Then make sure you know what you're getting in the data plan.

You should have a good idea of how much you use your phone to talk, text, surf the Web, and instant-message other people. However, it's best if you have more than a good idea when you're looking at a new data plan. Consider reviewing your last three months' bills and averaging out the number of text messages that you use each month, the number of data transfers that you use each month, and so on. And don't forget to factor in that your new G1 is specifically designed to surf the

5

Web, so you might spend more time doing some of those activities than you did in the past.

With your usage calculated, you can begin to look for plans. But beware: A data plan doesn't necessarily mean that you're getting web usage *and* messaging. Make sure you understand exactly what's included in the plan before you sign a contract. Some companies offer web usage and messaging as separate packages unless you're willing to shell out a pile of cash.

You can change service plans inside a contract, but it's never good to get that $500 phone bill because you thought all your messaging was included when it wasn't. Know what you're getting and avoid those nasty surprises.

Instead of risking a ridiculous bill, connect through the available wireless capability on your phone. It's easy. These steps should help you create the connection:

No Joke The following steps mention connecting to an unsecured wireless network. Always use caution when connecting to an unsecured network, especially on a handheld device that has minimal security. Any information on your device is wide open to hackers who are on the network and know how to access your device from their computers. It's always preferable to connect to a secure network that has a limited number of users.

1. Make sure you're within range of either a wireless network that has open security or one that you have the network key available to access.

2. From the **Home** screen on your device, press the **Menu** key and then touch **Settings**. Alternatively, you can open the applications menu and touch **Settings**.

3. This opens the Settings page. Touch **Wireless Controls**.

4. You are taken to the Wireless Controls page (refer to Figure 5.1).

5. You need to turn on your wireless capabilities so that your phone can connect with an available wireless network. Place a check mark in the checkbox to the right of **Wi-Fi** to turn on the Wi-Fi capabilities.

6. Alternatively, you can turn on the Wi-Fi capabilities by touching **Wi-Fi Settings** and then placing a check mark in the box next to **Wi-Fi** on

the Wi-Fi Settings page, shown in Figure 5.4. When you back out of this option using the **Back** key, you'll see that the **Wi-Fi** option on the previous screen is selected.

FIGURE 5.4

You can turn on Wi-Fi from within the Wi-Fi Settings screen.

7. When you select to enable Wi-Fi on the Wi-Fi Settings page, you should see a list of **Wi-Fi Networks** appear, as shown in Figure 5.5. Select your network.

Yellow Box

If you've never connected to your Wi-Fi network (or if you're connecting to a different network than your own) and your network is secured, you'll receive a connection prompt requesting the password for your network. You can select the **Show Password** option to show the characters of the password you're entering instead of hiding them. When you've entered the network password, touch **Connect** to create your network connection.

8. When you've created a network connection, you will automatically be connected to that network each time your device is in range and your Wi-Fi capabilities are enabled.

FIGURE 5.5

Select your wireless network from the list of available networks.

Sometimes your network doesn't appear on the list of available networks. This can occur when you've created a new network and the device has not yet recognized it. To set up a new or unrecognized network so that you can connect to it, use these steps:

1. If your network isn't showing as an available network on the Wi-Fi Networks list, you can always add it by scrolling to the end of the list and touching **Add a Wi-Fi Network**.

2. The Add a Wi-Fi Network form appears. Enter the network Service Set Identifier (SSID—that's the name of the network).

3. From the **Security** drop-down menu, select the network security type.

4. Touch **Save** to add the network to the list.

5. Connect to the network using the same steps you used to connect to other networks.

Connecting to the Wi-Fi network is really that easy, and it's your key to being able to surf the Web without running up massive data transfer charges. The best part is that free Wi-Fi hotspots are widely available—in coffeehouses, restaurants, hotels, and even some businesses. Now that you're connected, you can start surfing (and everything else that comes along with a Wi-Fi connection).

Understanding the Android Browser

One of the most anticipated applications on the Android platform is the web browser. Not surprisingly, many people are looking to Android and the Android phone to be a fully functional web device that offers a surfing experience close to that of a laptop or desktop.

With the release of the Google Chrome web browser just weeks before the official announcement of the Android phone, many experts believed that the web browser included with the Android phone would be a mobile version of Chrome that was quickly dubbed "Chrome Lite." That assumption wasn't entirely correct, but many people still refer to the browser as Chrome Lite.

The browser that's included with Android is actually built on an application called WebKit, which is an integral part of Google Chrome. WebKit is an open source rendering engine that enables the web browser to quickly scale and rescale a website to provide the most "normal" view of the Web possible on a mobile device. This means that when you pull up a web page on your Android phone, you see the actual page, not a scaled-down, mobile version of the page.

It also means that the Android phone loads web browser pages faster than most other mobile web devices because of the way WebKit renders the pages. It takes two passes at the pages, loading first the "easy" elements of the page and then the page elements that take longer to download. This gives you the appearance of a faster-loading page and enables you to surf with fewer interruptions.

Users have only one complaint about the web browser so far: It doesn't support Flash. However, it's believed that Google will add support for Flash during a future update, and it will most likely appear on future Android-based devices. Of course, this isn't the official word from Google or the Android developers, so it's also possible (although not likely) that Flash support will never be part of the Android web browser.

Accessing the Browser

To surf the Web, you must have an application that acts as an interface: a web browser. Having deep roots in web usability, Android comes equipped with a web browser that's fairly intuitive to use. Accessing the browser is easy: Simply touch the **Browser** icon on the Home screen, as shown in Figure 5.6.

If you've deleted your browser icon from the Home screen for some reason, you can also access it by opening the applications menu and then touching the **Browser** icon, as shown in Figure 5.7.

FIGURE 5.6

The Browser icon appears on the Home screen the first time you turn on your Android Phone.

FIGURE 5.7

A Browser icon is also located in the applications menu.

Browser Controls

When opening the web browser, a new page automatically loads. So far, it's close to the same browsing experience that you've always had on your desktop or laptop computer. Navigation is similar, but is controlled by finger gestures and the scroll ball on the device.

The first thing that you'll notice as you're navigating a page is that as soon as you start to move the page around, a small set of controls appears in the lower portion of the web page. These controls, shown in Figure 5.8, enable you to zoom in or out of a web page, and to shrink the page to select a portion of it instead of scrolling from top to bottom or left to right, as shown in Figure 5.9.

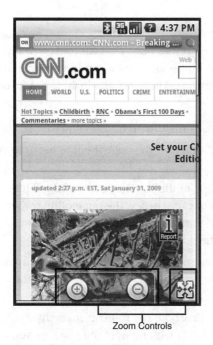

Zoom Controls

FIGURE 5.8

Zoom controls enable you to zoom in or out on any web page. The cross-hair selector enables you to shrink a page and select a specific area of it.

FIGURE 5.9

You can shrink a page and select a portion of that page to jump to instead of scrolling through the whole page.

When you touch either the plus or minus sign to zoom in or out on a page, you'll notice that most pages *reflow* automatically. This means the content on the page redistributes to fit within the browser window and reduces the amount of left-to-right scrolling needed. It works on most pages, but it's a useful feature in a web browser.

> *Reflow* means to redistribute. In the case of website content, reflowing occurs when a user zooms in or out on a page. The text is resized and redistributed to reduce the amount of right-to-left scrolling that is necessary to see all the content on the page. However, reflowing the page does make it longer, so it becomes necessary to scroll up and down more.

Link Menus

In addition to these onscreen controls, you have some touch and navigation options. For example, when you're on a web page that contains web links, you can touch a link to navigate to that page, or you can long-touch that link to open a new menu of available actions. Those actions include the following:

- **Open**—Opens the page.
- **Open in New Window**—Opens the link in a new window.
- **Bookmark Link**—Adds that link (not the page the link is on) to your bookmarks.
- **Save Link**—Downloads a copy of the link to your download history. After it's there, you can go back and access the page offline when you're ready to view it. Note that when you choose this option, graphics won't display on the page when you load it.
- **Share Link**—Sends the link to someone else using the email application that you have set up on your phone. You'll learn more about email on the Android Phone in Chapter 6, "Email Anywhere."
- **Copy Link URL**—Copies the link address. You can then enter it into the web browser when you're finished looking over the page, or you can open a second page to open the link in.

Multiple Page Instances

You might have noticed that we referred to opening additional web pages. The web browser on the Android Phone doesn't have the tab capabilities that you've probably become accustomed to with PC-based browsers. However, it does have the capability to open multiple web pages as separate instances, similar to tabbed browsing. The difference is in how you access those pages.

To open a separate instance of a web page, you can choose that option from the link menu, as mentioned previously. Or use the following option, which works best if you're not following a link:

1. With the web browser open, press the **Menu** key.

2. Touch the **Window** icon on the menu that appears. You move a **Current Windows** screen, shown in Figure 5.10.

FIGURE 5.10

Your open browser windows appear on this page. You can have up to eight browser windows open at a time.

3. Touch the **New Window** option. A new web page (also called a window) opens to your default home page.

4. To switch between the two windows, use the same steps to display the open windows and select the one you want to view.

You can open up to eight browser windows at a time. When you reach eight, you won't have the **New Window** option again until you close one of the pages.

To close a browser window that you no longer need, just open the **Window** option and then touch the **X** in the bottom-right corner of the page that you want to close.

Go to URL

When you pressed the Menu key from inside the browser, you probably noticed several other options. One of those options was **Go to URL**. When you touch this button, an address bar opens at the top of whatever web page you're on, as shown in Figure 5.11.

FIGURE 5.11

Type a web address into the address bar or select from the addresses that are shown in the drop-down menu.

Below the address bar, a drop-down menu appears. This menu contains a list of all the web addresses you've visited since the last time you cleared the browser cache. It's easier just to select the address you need from the list than to open the keyboard and type it again if you're visiting a web page that you've visited in the recent past.

Search

One of the neat features about the Android phone and other Android-based devices is that you have a search window available without needing to open a web browser. On the Android phone, the search window is on the right side of the Home screen. You can't see it all the time, but if you sweep your finger to the left, the page scrolls and you see the search box shown in Figure 5.12.

FIGURE 5.12

A Google search box is built into the Home screen of the Android phone; you just need to sweep your finger to the left side of the screen to find it.

But what if you're already surfing the Web and don't want to close out of the browser to have access to search? That option is available in the Browser menu. Just press the **Menu** key from within the browser and touch **Search**.

The page that you're currently viewing dims and a search box opens at the top of the screen. However, when you type your search term into the box and touch the **Search** key, the search results replace the web page that you were previously surfing. A new window doesn't open.

One cool feature of both search options is that suggestive search terms appear as you're typing, as shown in Figure 5.13. Just begin typing the term that you want to search for, and the search bar begins suggesting autofills that might be appropriate. If you see the search term you want in the suggested list of terms, just touch it to perform the search.

The search on an Android-based phone, even the Android phone, is Google based. This makes sense, because Google is the driving force behind Android. But the Google search engine is also one of the easiest to use, and it returns some of the best search results on the Web.

FIGURE 5.13

As you begin to type a term into the search bar, a list of suggested keywords and phrases appears. The list narrows as you type.

Bookmarks

As you surf the Web, you're sure to find pages that you want to return to at another time. The browser has a bookmark option that you can find by pressing the **Menu** key.

To add a bookmark, press the **Menu** key. Then when the **Bookmarks** menu shown in Figure 5.14 appears, touch the **New Bookmark** option.

The **Bookmark Link** window appears, as shown in Figure 5.15. Enter a **Name** for the bookmark if you don't want the one that's suggested, and then check the **Location** to be sure it's the URL you want to bookmark. If it's not, you can change it. When you're done, touch **OK** to save the bookmark.

One option that you won't find on the Bookmarks page is the option to manage your bookmarks—rearrange, edit, and delete them. You can edit and delete them, but you can't rearrange them. The order in which the bookmarks appear in the window is the order in which you've entered them, from oldest to newest, and that's the only order option that you have.

FIGURE 5.14

The Bookmarks page shows a list of the bookmarks you've created and an option for creating new bookmarks.

FIGURE 5.15

Use the Bookmark Link window to create a bookmark for the page that you're on or for any other page that you know the web address to.

However, you have options to edit or delete your bookmarks. You can find these capabilities in the individual menu for each bookmark. To get to that menu, long-press the bookmark that you want to change or delete. A menu such as the one shown in Figure 5.16 appears.

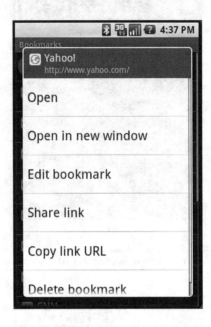

FIGURE 5.16

Each bookmarked link has an individual menu that enables you to open, edit, and delete the bookmark.

More options appear on this menu than just editing and deleting. The full list of menu options includes the following:

■ **Open**—Opens the bookmarked URL in the same browser window that you're currently using.

■ **Open in New Window**—Opens the bookmarked URL in a new browser window, preserving the browser window that you're currently using.

■ **Edit Bookmark**—Opens the Bookmark Link window to enable you to edit the name or URL of the bookmark.

■ **Share Link**—Opens a Gmail message to enable you to send the link to someone else. Enter the email address of the intended recipient, add a subject and body text if you want, and then touch **Send** to send the message with the link included.

- **Copy Link URL**—Copies the URL to the Clipboard so you can paste it in a different location.

- **Delete Bookmark**—Deletes the bookmark completely. When deleted, the only way to add back a bookmark is to re-create it from scratch. When you select the delete option, you receive a confirmation message before the bookmark is deleted completely.

One last option on the Bookmarks page that you might find useful is the capability to bookmark the last page you viewed. From the **Bookmarks** page, press the **Menu** key. The option **Bookmark Last-Viewed Page** comes up. Touch that option to open the **Bookmark Link** window. As with creating a new bookmark, the bookmark information is already filled in. All you have to do is ensure that it's correct.

Refresh

Some web pages change frequently. For example, if you're on a web-based email page, new emails might be coming in at any time. However, on most pages that have changing content, either you have to wait for the browser to refresh automatically—usually that option is scheduled to happen every few minutes—or you can refresh the page.

In the Android phone's web browser, you can refresh at any time by selecting the **Refresh** option from the browser menu. Just touch the option and the page reloads. Then any changes appear that have taken place on the page since the last time it automatically refreshed or since you entered the page.

Additional Browser Options

One last option on the browser menu is the **More** icon. When you open the More option, it brings up a whole new menu (or submenu) of available options, as shown in Figure 5.17. Those options include the following:

- **Back**—Takes you back to the previous page.

- **Forward**—If you navigated back to a previous page, returns you to the last page.

- **Home Page**—Takes you to your home page.

- **History**—Shows a history of the pages you've visited. You can clear the history by pressing the **Menu** key while on the history page. The **Clear History** option appears; touch it to delete your entire history.

- **Downloads**—Takes you to a page that displays your download history. Touch any one of the files to go to that file, or press the **Menu** key to open the options to **Clear List** or **Cancel Download** (if a download is in progress).

- **Page Info**—Shows the title and web address of the page you're currently visiting. This information opens in a pop-up window. When you're done viewing it, touch **OK** to close the window.

- **Bookmark Page**—Takes you to the New Bookmark page that you saw previously. This is just an alternative way to bookmark web pages.

- **Share Page**—Opens a Gmail message with the URL for the current page included. Enter an email address, add a subject and any body text that you want to add, and then press **Send** to send the message with the link included.

- **Flip Orientation**—Changes the orientation of the browser from landscape to portrait. You can also accomplish the same task by opening the slide-out keyboard. However, when you use the **Flip Orientation** option in this menu to display the browser in landscape mode, it remains that way even when the keyboard is closed.

- **Zoom**—Opens the zoom controls for the web page. You can access the same controls by moving the page with your finger.

FIGURE 5.17

Additional browser options give you more navigation capabilities when surfing the Web.

Settings

A whole world of options is available in the **Settings** option within the **More** option of the browser menu.

An extensive menu appears when you touch the Settings option. It enables you to make adjustments to Page Content settings, Privacy settings, Security settings, and Advanced settings.

Page Content Settings

Page Content settings are pretty basic. The first option you have is **Text Size**. This enables you to adjust the text on a displayed web page to **Tiny**, **Small**, **Normal**, **Large**, or **Huge**. Just touch the text size that you want to use and then touch **OK** to set it. You might want to play with it to find the size that works best for you.

Your next option is **Block Pop-Up Windows**. Just place a check mark in the checkbox to the right of the option to turn on pop-up blocking, or remove the check mark to turn it off. Some websites require you to disable pop-up blocking to interact with the site, but we recommend that you keep pop-up blocking enabled unless you're on a site for which you know you need to disable it.

Phishers and other cybercriminals often use pop-ups to load malware to your system or to entice you to provide personal information that they use to commit identity theft.

Phishers are cybercriminals that "fish" around trying to collect bits and pieces of your personal information for the purposes of stealing your identity. These criminals might use emails to entice you to send personal information such as usernames and passwords, or even credit card or banking information online. When you do, the criminal collects it, resells it to someone else, who uses it for their own personal financial gain, no matter what the cost to you.

Load Images is another option in the Page Content settings. This option determines whether images on web pages are automatically loaded. For the best web experience, enable Load Images; for the fastest experience, disable it.

In the past, surfing the Web on a mobile device was a painful process because you got either scaled-down pages meant for mobile surfing or pages that weren't made to display on small screens. The reflowing capability of the Android phone makes surfing the Web on your device a more pleasant experience. However, if you don't want pages that are automatically scaled to fit your screen, you can manage that feature through the **Auto-Fit Pages** option. Turn on the option to reflow pages to your device size; turn it off to show the original size of the page. Just be aware that with the Auto-Fit option turned off, you need to do a lot more left-to-right scrolling.

The capability to access JavaScript content in the browser is another Android phone feature that makes surfing the web more enjoyable. JavaScript content provides richer capabilities when searching online. However, some people worry that it can be a security risk. If you're one of those people, you can turn JavaScript off (or back on) using the **Enable JavaScript** option.

As you're navigating the Web, you might find it frustrating that pages opening in a new window appear in front of the page you were surfing on. Remember that you can switch between windows. You can also enable the **Open in Background** option to open new windows behind the page that you're currently visiting. This enables you to finish your surfing on the page that you're viewing before you're forced to move on to the next window.

The last option in the Page Content settings window is **Set Home Page**. If you have a favorite website that you want to use as your home page, you can set that up here. Just touch the option, and the **Set Home Page** window appears, as shown in Figure 5.18. Type the URL of the web page that you want to use as your home page into the box provided and select **OK** to save it. The next time you open your browser, you'll be taken to that page instead of the default home page.

FIGURE 5.18

Enter the URL for the web page that you want to use as your home page, and touch OK to save it.

Privacy Settings

Privacy is a big deal on the Internet, including the mobile web. You don't want other people to have access to your personal information or be able to track your movements while you're online.

The first three options in the Privacy Settings section of the Settings menu—Clear Cache, Clear History, and Accept Cookies—are options that you can use to protect your privacy. Touch **Clear Cache** and **Clear History** to remove past web pages and cookies from your browser cache. This makes it harder for others to track your movements online.

Enable or disable **Accept Cookies** to accept or decline cookie data. Cookies are small snippets of data that websites place in your browser cache to help them recognize you when you navigate to them. This is how Amazon.com always knows who you are, even when you're not technically signed into your account. It's also how many websites remember your personalization settings, and how they know what pages you visit while you're on their site. Declining cookies removes some of the personalization from your browsing experience, but it also keeps you safe if you're worried about your online movements being tracked.

If you want to clear your cookie data, you can select the **Clear All Cookie Data** option. This opens a confirmation window. Select **OK** to clear the data or **Cancel** to return to the Settings menu without clearing the data.

The final two options in this section of the menu relate to form data. Form data is the information that you enter into forms on the Web. This includes your name, usernames, passwords, addresses, and other information that might be requested when you're filling out a form online.

Entering that information from a mobile device can be time consuming, so the browser has the option to **Remember Form Data**. Select this option to enable it, or deselect to disable it. If you deselect the option, you'll need to enter form data each time you encounter a form.

You can clear the form data at any time by selecting the **Clear Form Data** option. When you touch this option, a confirmation window appears prompting you to confirm that you want to clear the data. Touch **OK** to clear it and **Cancel** to return to the settings menu.

Security Settings

You'll find only three options in the Security Settings section of the menu. Two of these options relate to passwords. You can choose to remember website passwords by selecting the **Remember Passwords** options, or you can turn off this option by deselecting it.

5

Because passwords change, you might need to clear the passwords that you have stored and reenter them. Touch the **Clear Passwords** option to remove all the passwords that you have stored. The next time you enter a password-protected website, you'll be prompted to enter your password again. But if you have the **Remember Passwords** option enabled, you won't be prompted to enter it on subsequent visits. Also, you'll receive a confirmation message before the passwords are cleared. Touch **OK** to clear the passwords and **Cancel** to return to the menu without clearing them.

The other option in Security Settings is **Show Security Warnings**. If this option is enabled and you try to enter a website that has problems with a security certificate, you'll see a warning about the site. When it's disabled, you'll receive no warnings. If you want to be sure that you always know the website you're surfing is safe, leave this option enabled.

Advanced Settings

The last section of the Settings menu includes three advanced settings that you might find useful. Two of the settings relate to Google Gears, a browser extension that enables developers to create browser-based applications that can run offline. For example, some databases can run within a browser, but Google Gears can make it possible to run that database within the browser, even when your device is not signed in online.

To enable or disable Google Gears on your device, touch the **Enable Gears** option. The other Gears option is **Gears Settings**. Touch this option to open a window that shows a table of the sites that you have granted permission to use Gears. At this time, Gears isn't commonly used, so your list might be small or even nonexistent (see Figure 5.19). In the future, however, as more developers take advantage of Gears, that list will grow.

The last option in the Settings menu is **Reset to Default**. This option clears all your browser data—including bookmarks, passwords, and all the settings that you have personalized—and returns everything to the original settings that your browser had when you first turned on the device. Use this option only if you're sure that you want to completely reset your browser. When you touch the **Reset to Default** option, you'll receive a confirmation message. Select **OK** to reset everything and **Cancel** to return to the Settings page.

The browser has more capabilities than you might expect when you first open it. But because Android is designed to take full advantage of the Web on a mobile level, you should expect no less. Still, some people find that the browser isn't quite what they're looking for. For those people, Opera Mini is

available in Android Market as an alternative to the browser that's preinstalled on the G1. If you're an Opera user, you might be more comfortable
with the Mini than with the Android browser.

FIGURE 5.19
*The Gears Settings window shows a table of the websites that you have enabled to use Gears
on your device.*

Closing the Door

Whew! We've given you a lot of browser information. You can start surfing the
Web the instant you turn on your phone, but so many customization options
exist and so many navigation controls are available that it can take a little
time to get everything set up the way you're most comfortable using it.

Now that you've set up the browser to work the way you want it to, it's time to
have a little fun. In the next chapter, we look at the email capabilities of your
Android phone. Those capabilities include Gmail, but you can also access
other web-based email programs. You'll learn how in Chapter 6.

Email Anywhere

Of all the activities you'll conduct while you're online, email is likely the one you'll do most. According to some estimates, 1.3 billion email users send 210 billion emails each day. That's an astounding number of messages flying through the ether of the Internet.

If you're using an Android-enabled phone, you're probably using it to send and receive email messages. Fortunately, the Android phone has multiple email capabilities. You can use Gmail, which is probably the best option with the Android phone, or you can enable other web-based email services from the Android phone.

Introduction to Gmail

Google. Android. Gmail. The three terms just seem to go together. If you're using the Android-based phone, you're likely a fan of Google and you're probably already using Gmail. But if you're not, this section might convince you that you're missing out.

From the start, Gmail was purely web based. It has been a favored web mail application since its release in April 2004 (on April Fool's Day, to be exact). Many people originally came to Gmail seeking unlimited storage space. They stayed for the features, which seem to grow all the time.

Gmail seems to be in a perpetual state of beta testing. Even now, more than five years after its first release, Gmail still has the beta indicator attached to its logo. That's because Gmail is constantly changing. Unlimited storage became limited, although the limits are tremendously high. I currently have more than 38,000 emails stored in my Gmail account, dating back to August 2004, and have not yet reached the 50% mark on my storage limits.

Over time, Google has added other capabilities to Gmail—chat through Google Talk, Google Calendar, Google Docs, and even themes. Google also has created mobile versions of Gmail—and that's where the Android phone comes in.

Gmail on mobile phones is fairly simple to use. It has a straightforward interface and gives you access to the most important controls. But as good as the mobile version is (for what it is), it doesn't provide the same mobile experience that you get with an Android-based phone. Again, because all this is associated with Google, the best options for productivity, communications, and access are those Google offers.

Accessing Gmail

When you first started the Android phone and signed into it using a Google account, you were asked to enter a username and password. If you're a Gmail user, your username and password were probably the same as your Gmail account username and password. Accessing Gmail thus is as easy as opening the applications menu and touching the Gmail icon, shown in Figure 6.1.

FIGURE 6.1
Select the Gmail icon to open your Gmail account.

If you created a Google account but didn't create a Gmail account, you can quickly and easily set one up. These steps walk you through it:

Yellow Box

You can create a Gmail account from either your phone or your desktop or laptop computer. If your desktop or laptop computer is handy, we recommend using it because you can more easily enter the requested information using a keyboard and mouse than using the slide-out keyboard of the Android phone. Also, the account-creation page doesn't scale well on the Android phone, making it more difficult to move through the form.

1. Open your browser and go to www.gmail.com.

2. Click the **Sign Up for Gmail** link on the right side of the page. The account-creation page loads.

3. Enter your name, the login name you want to use, a password, a security question and answer, and a secondary email (this is optional) into the form provided (see Figure 6.2). A security verification and terms of service acknowledgment are also required.

6

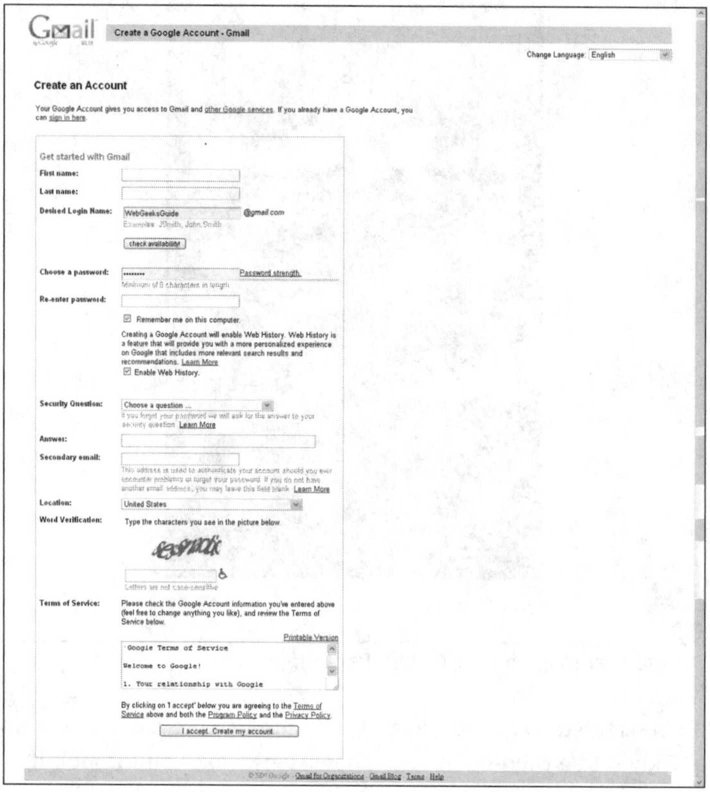

FIGURE 6.2

Provide the requested information to create a Gmail account that you can access with your G1.

4. Click **Continue**. A new page loads and shows some of the basic information you need to know about your account.

5. After you've read the information, click **I'm Ready—Show Me My Account**. Your Gmail account page loads and you're automatically signed in (see Figure 6.3).

After you've created your Gmail account, you can log into it with your Android-based device by touching the **Gmail** icon from the applications menu.

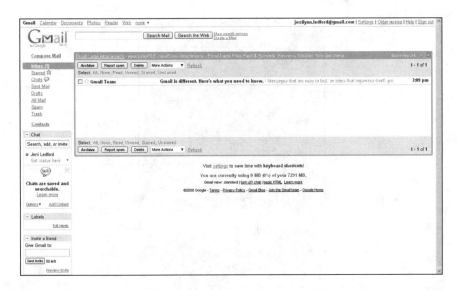

FIGURE 6.3
The first time you log into your Gmail account, you'll see a Welcome message from the Gmail team and your basic account controls.

Using Gmail to Send and Receive Messages

Using Gmail on your Android-enabled phone is easy. To access your messages, simply touch the **Gmail** icon in the applications menu. That takes you to your Gmail page, shown in Figure 6.4.

Reading Messages

You'll see two types of messages displayed on this screen: messages that you've read and messages that you haven't. The messages you've read appear in normal typeface. Those you haven't read are displayed in bold.

To read a message, touch the message subject. The message appears onscreen with one important security function. Even messages that have embedded images do not automatically display the images. As Figure 6.5 shows, when a message has images to display, a **Preview** button appears. Touch the button to display the images.

FIGURE 6.4

When you open your Gmail account, you'll see your messages displayed onscreen. Unread messages are bold.

FIGURE 6.5

Messages are displayed with images disabled so that they load faster and protect you from embedded malware. Touch the button to display images.

Messages that are text only also display differently than messages with images embedded in them. A text-only message scales to display on your device screen, whereas messages that have images embedded in them don't. This means you have to do more scrolling to see the included images.

Receiving Messages

If you have set up your device to synchronize with email, Gmail should automatically update each time you receive a new message. (If you don't remember covering syncing your device, flip back to Chapter 3, "Basic Use of Your Android Phone"—we cover this in the "To Sync or Not to Sync" section near the end of the chapter.)

When you have Gmail open, the message updates on the screen and a notification tone sounds. When you're in any other application or on the home screen, a notification tone sounds and the @ sign appears in the Notification area of your phone.

To access Gmail from the message notification, open the window-shade notification area, shown in Figure 6.6, and touch the email notification. This takes you to your Gmail inbox.

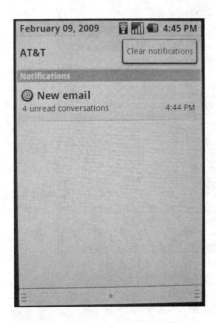

FIGURE 6.6
To go to your Gmail inbox, touch the notification icon in the window-shade notification area.

If you're in your Gmail box and you want to know if you've received any new messages before signing out, you can refresh the page. Press the **Menu** key and then touch **Refresh**. The page loads briefly; you can see any changes immediately.

Composing and Sending Messages

Email isn't simply about the messages you receive. It also involves responses that you send and the new messages that you create. With Gmail mobile, sending a message response is simple; you just have to be able to find the message controls (and sometimes those aren't immediately obvious).

When you open a message in Gmail, the header and body of the message appear on your screen. Unless the message is short, that's probably all you'll see. But if you scroll farther down the page by dragging your finger up the screen, you'll see the controls that enable you to reply to a message (see Figure 6.7).

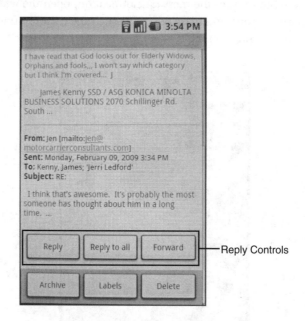

FIGURE 6.7

The controls you need to reply to an existing message are at the bottom of the message. You might have to scroll down to see them.

To reply to the person who sent you the message, touch the **Reply** button. If the message included more than one person in the recipient string, you can reply to everyone in the string by touching the **Reply to All** button, or you can forward the message to another person by touching the **Forward** button.

Touching any one of these three buttons opens a mail form. When you touch Reply or Reply to All, you'll see that the recipient field is already filled out, and your cursor appears in the message field for you to add your own text.

When you choose the Forward option, the new message appears just like before, except that your cursor automatically moves to the **To** field so that you can add recipients to the message.

When you're finished composing your message, touch the **Send** option at the bottom of the page (you'll probably have to scroll down to get to it). If you're not ready to send the message, you also have the options **Save As Draft** or **Discard**. If you choose to save the message as a draft, you'll be able to find it in the **Draft** folder.

If you want to send a new message that is not a reply to another or a forward of another, you can do that, too. You must be in the Inbox to compose a new message. From the Inbox, use these steps to send a new message:

1. Press the **Menu** key to open a menu of additional functions (shown in Figure 6.8).

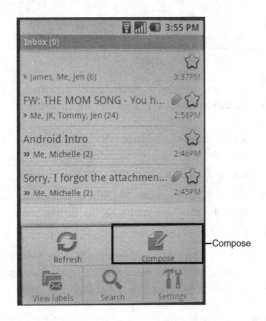

FIGURE 6.8

Press the Menu key to open a menu of available email options, including Compose.

2. Touch **Compose** to open a new mail form.

3. The new mail form opens, with your cursor in the **To** field. Enter the email address of the person you want to send the message to. The To field has an autocomplete option, based on the email addresses you have in your address book (see Figure 6.9). If the address you want to use appears in this list, touch it to add it automatically.

FIGURE 6.9

An autocomplete function provides suggested email addresses that you might be typing. If the address you want is shown, touch it to add it to the message.

4. If you want to add more than one email address, begin typing the next one. The autocomplete options appear again. Use the same actions you did in step 3 to add another address.

5. When you've entered the email address (or addresses) that you want to send the message to, touch the **Subject** line to add a message subject.

6. Touch the body of the message to enter the text of the message.

7. When you've finished composing the message and you're ready to send it, touch the **Send** button at the bottom of the screen. Alternatively, you can select **Save As Draft** or **Discard**.

It's also possible to add an attachment to messages that you send from your Android phone. In fact, you can access a whole group of additional commands when you're within the Compose Message screen. To reach those commands, press the **Menu** key (while you're in the Compose Message screen). This brings up a menu of available commands, including these:

- **Send**—Sends the message.
- **Add Cc/Bcc**—Opens additional copy and blind copy address fields, as shown in Figure 6.10.

FIGURE 6.10
Use the Cc and Bcc fields to add copy and blind copy recipients for your message.

- **Attach**—Opens the picture file so you can select a picture to send to someone. Touch the picture that you want to include to attach it to the message. You're then returned to the Compose screen. If you change your mind about attaching the picture, touch the X to the right of the filename to remove it. Unfortunately, the only option that you have for attaching files is to select a picture.
- **Edit Subject**—Moves your cursor back to the subject line so you can edit it.
- **Discard**—Discards the message.

Yellow Box

When you're working with text, you might think you can use certain finger motions, but the motions don't always work as expected. For example, you might expect to be able to select a word or line of text by sweeping your finger over it. But that doesn't work. To select text (also called highlighting it), press the **Shift** key on the keyboard while moving the track ball to the left or right. Alternatively, you can long-touch a selection of text and choose **Select All**. To copy the text, use a long touch and select **Copy** from the menu that appears. To paste the text somewhere else, place the cursor where you want to the text to go and long-touch that area of the screen; select **Paste** when it appears onscreen. You can learn more about keyboard shortcuts in Appendix B, "G1 Keyboard Shortcuts."

Advanced Gmail Controls

Already Gmail Mobile is a pretty comprehensive application. It's missing a few capabilities (such as the capability to attach something besides a picture to your message), but these likely will be added with future updates to Android. In the meantime, you can still do a lot with Gmail, especially to organize and manage your email.

Managing Your Email

You probably get dozens, if not hundreds, of email messages a day. With that volume of email coming in, you have to stay organized. Fortunately, Gmail offers some good organization options.

One way to manage your email is to use labels. Labels allow you to separate messages using indicators that make it easy for you to find a specific message or group of messages. For example, you can set up a label for all the messages that come to you from a specific person. Then, to see all of those communications, just select that label. You can use labels for just about any topic imaginable, too.

From your Inbox (which is a label, too), press the **Menu** key and then touch **View Labels** to see a list of the labels that are available for your mail. Now, here's the frustrating part about labels: You can't create them from Gmail Mobile—either the Gmail Mobile application that's installed on your phone or the mobile version of Gmail through your web browser. To create labels, you must log onto Gmail through a web browser; if you're using the mobile browser on your device, you must scroll to the bottom of the page (after you log in) and touch the **Desktop** link beneath **View Gmail In**.

When the new version of Gmail loads, you'll see a drastic difference. This is the Gmail that you see when you're using your laptop or desktop computer. Scroll over the right side of the screen and touch the **Settings** link. Then touch the **Labels** link near the top of the Settings box.

A new page loads with a list of labels that are available for your emails. At the bottom of the list is a text box labeled **Create a New Label**. Type the name of the label that you want to create and then touch the **Create** button. The page reloads and the new label appears in the list. You can repeat these steps to create as many labels as you need.

If you're using the Android browser to create new labels, you might not see the other fields that are available for labels. As you can see in Figure 6.11, to the right of the label names, you also have some options for renaming labels, removing labels, and showing labels in IMAP. IMAP is the messaging protocol, so if you don't want specific labels to show up in Gmail Mobile, you can deselect them here to keep them from appearing.

FIGURE 6.11
Use the options in Gmail's desktop view to change, delete, and hide email labels.

Back on your mobile device, when you log into Gmail either through your browser or through the Gmail Mobile application, you then can use labels to organize your email messages.

No Joke Don't forget to switch back to the normal view of Gmail in your mobile browser when you're done editing labels. Using the normal view (which, for a mobile device, is actually the mobile view) makes it much easier to navigate.

When you open a message and want to archive the message in one of the folders you've created (labels are actually folders), press the **Menu** key (from within the open message) and touch **Change Labels**. A list of the available labels appears, as shown in Figure 6.12.

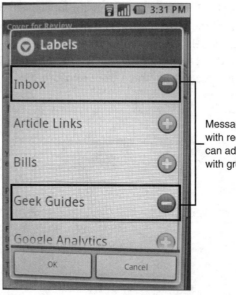

Message is assigned to folders with red circles but you can add it to folders with green circles

FIGURE 6.12

Choose from the list of available labels to determine how the message should be archived. A message can have more than one label.

The label that shows the red circle with a dash in it is the one the message is currently using. The other labels (with green circles that have plus marks) are available. Touch any of them to change that circle to the red one. If you change your mind, you can touch the label again to change it back to green. Labels with the red mark appear on the message, and you can have more than one label per message.

If you want to change the label you've assigned to a message, first open the message that you want to change, press the **Menu** key, and touch **Change**

Label. The list of labels appears. Touch the label (or labels) that you want to use and then touch **OK**. Remember that you also have to touch the label that is currently displayed on the message to remove it.

Another method of organizing your email messages is to use the **Star** option with them. Starring a message causes a yellow star to appear on the message, and then the message is filed in the **Starred** folder when you archive it.

If you star a message and later want to unstar it, you can open the message, press the **Menu** key, and touch **Remove Star**. This puts the message back in the **All Mail** category; if the message had any other labels, it will appear in those folders as well.

We've mentioned *archiving* a message. When you archive a message, you remove the message from the inbox without deleting it. If the message has a label on it, it is archived in the folder that corresponds to that label (or multiple folders, if it has multiple labels). If the message has no label, it is archived in the **All Mail** folder, along with every other message that you've received and archived, but not deleted.

Deleted messages appear in the **Trash** folder, spam messages appear in the **Spam** folder, and messages that you've sent to other people appear in the **Sent** folder. To archive a message, open the message and then press the **Menu** key. In the menu that appears, touch **Archive** to archive the message. The message is removed from the inbox but appears in the folder for whatever label was designated, or in the **All Mail** folder if you did not assign a label.

A few more interesting email controls are the **Search** option, the **Mark As Unread** option, and the **Report Spam** option.

You can get to the **Search** option from your inbox. Just press the **Menu** key and select **Search**. This opens a Gmail search box at the top of the screen, as shown in Figure 6.13. Type in your search term and touch the **Search** button to see a list of results.

The search works for terms in the subject and body of the message, and also for names and specific email addresses. If you don't like to label your messages, you can still find the message using the search capabilities provided.

If you have a message that you want to keep as being unread even though you've already read it, you can mark it as unread. Open the message, press the **Menu** key, and then touch **Mark As Unread**. This returns you to the Inbox, and the message is displayed in bold typeface to show that it has not yet been read. Many people use this option for action items; an unread message begs to be read and acted upon.

6

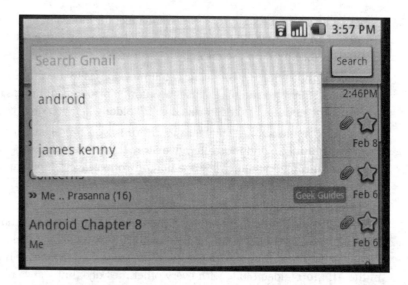

FIGURE 6.13

Use the search box to search your Gmail messages for a specific term or sender.

Finally, sometimes spam messages escape the Google spam filter. (It's good, but it's not perfect.) If you find a message that's spam, you can help the filter catch future messages of that type or messages from that domain by marking the message as spam. Open the message and press the **Menu** key. In the menu that appears, touch the **More** option. A small menu opens, containing two items: **Back to Inbox** and **Report Spam**.

If you touch **Report Spam**, the message is sent to your spam folder and removed from your inbox. In the future, messages that are similar to that one or that are from the same sender automatically will go into the spam folder.

Email Settings

Customizing your email in Gmail goes further than just labels and organization. A group of settings give you access to signatures and notification settings.

To access the settings for your email box, start in the Inbox. Press the **Menu** key and touch **Settings**. A Settings page like the one shown in Figure 6.14 appears.

You have two categories of settings: **General Settings** and **Notification Settings**.

FIGURE 6.14
The Settings option enables you to further customize your Gmail mobile account.

General Settings

In General settings, you'll find two available options, Labels and Signature. You've already seen the Labels option, but here it isn't used to assign labels or view messages that you've labeled.

Here, the **Labels** option enables you to decide which labels you want to sync when your Gmail account syncs up. To sync with any label shown, touch it. A **Sync All** notation appears to the right of the label to indicate that all the messages in that folder will be synced during the next syncing process.

To sync only recently added items, touch the same label a second time. To remove syncing capabilities from the label, touch it a third time (or until the label line shows no sync notification).

When you're done, press the **Back** key to return to the Settings page.

The other option you have in General Settings is the Signature option. When you touch the **Signature** option, a pop-up window appears, as shown in Figure 6.15. Type the message that you want to appear in the textbox provided, and then touch **OK** to save the signature. Keep in mind that you have no fancy formatting options, so signatures appear as plain messages appended to the end of your email. These messages will be added to all your outgoing messages.

FIGURE 6.15

In the box provided, type the text that you want to appear in your signature. You can use multiple lines but no fancy formatting.

Notification Settings

The other settings options govern how you're notified when new emails arrive. The first setting is **Email Notifications**. Placing a check mark in the box next to **Email Notifications** notifies you through the status bar when new emails arrive. To stop receiving notifications, deselect this option.

The next option is **Select Ringtone**. Touching **Select Ringtone** brings up the Select a Ringtone menu. Touch one of the selections to hear the sound played. When you've found the sound that you want to set as the tone played when an email message comes in, touch **OK**. Your choice is saved and you're returned to the Settings page. If you decide not to change the tone, touch **Cancel** to keep your current settings and return to the Settings page.

The last notification option is to have your device vibrate when an email message comes through. To enable this option, place a check mark in the box to the right of **Vibrate**. Then each time a message comes through, your phone sounds a tone and vibrates (if you have set those options). You can deselect this option by removing the check mark from the box.

We've covered a lot of information about Gmail for your Android phone. But Gmail is meant to work well on a Mobile platform, and there's no better mobile platform for it than Android. Using them together gives you a full-service email account that helps you stay organized while you're communicating.

Other Email Services

We think Gmail works great for mobile devices, but not everyone will like it. You might prefer to use a different email service. The other email option on the Android phone works with just about any available web-based email application. You can set up most of those accounts automatically in a couple steps.

To set up an email account, follow these steps:

1. From the applications menu, touch **Email**.

2. A welcome message appears. Read the message and touch **Next**.

3. Enter the **Email Address** and **Password** information in the space provided for the account that you want to set up. Then touch **Next**.

4. The application attempts to set up your account automatically. In most cases, this succeeds the first time. If the application prompts you to enter the account settings manually, the email service that you're trying to set up should have a document available that lists the correct manual settings to apply.

5. When you've established the account, a setup screen appears, similar to the one shown in Figure 6.16. Enter a name for the account and then touch **Next**. On the next screen you'll be prompted to type your name as you want it displayed on outgoing emails. Then touch **Done**.

Now your email account is set up. In most cases, the process really is that easy. You then move to the inbox for the account. But that's not where your message and customization capabilities end.

When you're in the Inbox, you have many of the same capabilities that you saw earlier with Gmail. Press the **Menu** key to open a menu of options:

- **Refresh**—Refreshes your view of the inbox to see if you've received additional messages.

- **Compose**—Opens a blank email to compose and send.

- **Accounts**—Takes you back to your account view, where you can interact with the different accounts you've created. Long-touch an account name to open a menu of options for that account.

- **Account Settings**—Enables you to adjust settings for the account in which you are viewing the menu.

FIGURE 6.16

Give your email account a name, and add your password, then select Next to continue setup.

Account Settings

You can use the **Account Settings** option to make adjustments to the default settings for your email account. Touching **Account Settings** brings up a menu of settings. These include **General Settings**, **Notification Settings**, and **Server Settings**.

The first option under **General Settings** is **Account Name**. Touch **Account Name** to open a pop-up window where you can create or edit the name that you want this account displayed under. When you're done entering the name in the box provided, touch **OK** to save the name and return to the settings page.

The next option is **Your Name**. As with the Account Name, this opens a pop-up window where you can set or change the name that you want to have displayed on your outgoing emails.

Use the **Email Check Frequency** option to adjust how often your email is checked automatically from your device. By default, the frequency is set to **Never**, but you can change that by touching the option and then touching the frequency that you want to use. Frequencies start at every five minutes and increase incrementally to every hour. When you're satisfied with your selection, touch **OK** to save the setting and return to the menu.

The last setting in the General Settings section is **Default Account**. If you select this option, this becomes your default account for sending email. If you prefer to use another account, deselect this option.

Next up are **Notification Settings**. In this section of the settings page, you'll find the same notification settings that you saw in Gmail: **Email Notifications**, **Select Ringtone**, and **Vibrate**.

The Email Notifications and Vibrate Selection options are simply check boxes. For Select Ringtone, a pop-up window opens from which you can choose the ringtone that you want to use with this email account. One nice thing about this setting is that if you have multiple email addresses, you can set a different ringtone for each so that you know which email address is getting mail anytime an email comes through.

Yellow Box

The notification tones that are available on the Android phone are pretty limited. And the tones that you can download for the Android phone tend to be pretty lame. But that's okay. An application called Ringdroid lets you create your own notification tones (and ring-tones) from your favorite songs. You can find Ringdroid through the Android Marketplace.

The last section of the settings page is for **Server Settings**. These settings are the settings that were used to set up your account. They include **Incoming Settings** and **Outgoing Settings**.

If your account was set up automatically, you probably don't need to adjust these settings. If for some reason you need to, though, you'll find settings that cover incoming mail servers, outgoing mail servers, ports, and security types in these areas. I recommend that you work with these only if you know what your mail settings should be—if you enter the wrong setting, you could disable mobile access to the account.

6

One last setting in this section isn't really a server setting. **Add Another Account** takes you to a form like the one that you filled in to set up your first email account. You can use this option to add other email accounts if you have more than one web-based account that you want to access with your device.

You also might want to be familiar with the **Accounts** option. Touching **Accounts** takes you to a list of your email accounts, as shown in Figure 6.17. Long-touch any account that's listed to open a menu of options that includes **Open, Account Settings,** and **Remove Account.** You can open the account to view the inbox or account page, jump to the account settings, or delete the account if you no longer use it.

FIGURE 6.17

The Accounts option opens a list of the email accounts that you have set up. You can interact with these accounts using long touches.

Message Controls

In addition to account controls, you can access some message controls from within an email message. When you have an email message open, press the **Menu** key to open an additional menu of actions:

- **Delete**—Deletes the message
- **Forward**—Opens a forwarding message that you can address, add text to, and send
- **Reply**—Opens a reply message
- **Reply All**—Opens a reply message addressed to all recipients
- **Mark As Unread**—Marks the message as unread and returns you to the inbox

Of course, a message that you're composing also has additional controls, just as you learned with Gmail. To access those controls, press the **Menu** key from within a message you're composing. A menu of options opens:

- **Add Cc/Bcc**—Opens fields in the outgoing email so you can add recipients to be copied or blind-copied
- **Send**—Sends the message
- **Save As Draft**—Saves the message as a draft
- **Discard**—Discards the message without saving a draft
- **Add Attachment**—Opens the Pictures file so that you can attach a picture to the message

The controls for email accounts set up through the email option are much the same as the controls for Gmail accounts. However, you'll find that you don't have as much control over these accounts. Still, if you're not a Gmail user and you don't want to become one, you don't have to be without email. This is a good option for adding accounts that you might have in addition to your Gmail account.

Closing the Door

Email is a requirement for most people these days—and mobile email is quickly becoming a requirement. Fortunately, the Android phone has two options for email. Gmail, the first option, works well with the Android platform, giving you an email solution that's not only useful, but also pretty powerful in mobile terms.

But if you're not a Gmail user and you don't want to become one, you're not left out in the cold. A second email option enables you to set up email accounts from other providers. The controls for those accounts also are similar to the controls in Gmail; you just don't get all the functionality.

6

Now that you know how to manage your email, we can move on to something else. The next chapter delves into Google Maps and how it works with the Android-based Android phone. We also look at the GPS capabilities of the device more closely, so keep reading—we've got a lot of interesting stuff in store for you.

6

Getting Around with GPS and Google Maps

One of G1's most anticipated promises was the phone's Global Positioning Satellite (GPS) capabilities and accompanying location services. That's hardly surprising, considering that GPS units were one of the hottest Christmas gifts for 2008.

The uses for a GPS are limitless. Finding directions and pinpointing location are common uses, but less common ones include social networking and event routing. The buzz before the G1's release was more of a question: Would it include GPS capabilities, and how would they work with Android?

The good news is, yes, GPS was included first on the G1 and later on the myTouch. The better news is that the GPS's location capabilities are integrated with Google Maps and can be integrated with other (third-party) applications, making the GPS very usable. Still, the GPS has a few less-than-stellar aspects, which we cover in the "Other GPS Capabilities" section, later in this chapter.

An Introduction to the G1's GPS Capabilities

In Chapter 5, "Going Online," we covered enabling and disabling the Android phone's GPS capabilities. But there's more to GPS than just how to turn on a device.

We start with a short explanation of what GPS is and what it's intended for. Global Positioning Satellite (GPS) is a network of 24 satellites that orbit the globe at a tightly controlled rate of speed. Each satellite makes two orbits around the Earth each day.

These are important facts because the application of GPS is *location servicing*. For example, a GPS unit can pinpoint your location on a map based on the position of your GPS receiver relative to the nearest GPS satellites.

geek speak   Location servicing simply means providing a location. Location servicing works with GPS by sending a signal from a GPS device or a GPS satellite to a receiver. A mathematical equation determines the location of the receiver based on certain variables (such as how long it took to receive the signal).

The GPS system on your phone is a GPS receiver, which means that it can receive signals from the GPS satellites that are orbiting the planet. This has wide-reaching applications, including mapping, social networking, location servicing (such as finding your teenager when he's out on Saturday night), and dozens of other applications.

For the Android phones, the main application of GPS is in the Google Maps application (although that's not the *only* application). Google Maps for the Android-enabled device are tied to the GPS system, so you can pinpoint your current location and get directions from that point to wherever you want to go. As you've come to expect with Google applications, you can do more with Google Maps on the Android phones than just view maps.

Using Google Maps

Many people use Google Maps online; it's one of the "go-to" websites for directions. If you perform a search for a location such as a business through Google's search engine, you'll probably find a link to Google Maps as one of the top search results, as shown in Figure 7.1.

With Google Maps online, you're limited to creating a beginning and ending point to get directions that you can print or download. With Google Maps on your Android-enabled device, you can do more.

Google Maps Link

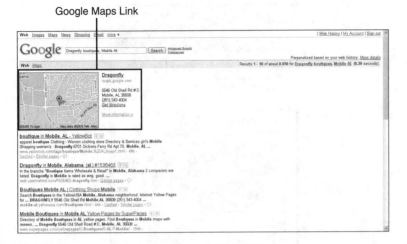

FIGURE 7.1

Links to Google Maps online appear in search results when you're searching for a location through the Google search engine.

No Joke   Before you start working with Google Maps on your Android-enabled device, make sure that your GPS system is enabled. Without the GPS, maps will still work, but you won't get as rich of an experience using Google Maps. If you don't remember how to enable or disable GPS on your Android phone, flip back to Chapter 5 for instructions.

Getting Directions

Let's start with searching for a location online. In Figure 7.1, I searched for "Dragonfly Boutiques, Mobile, AL." I can also search for that same term using Google's search function on my Android phone. The search results look a little different, as shown in Figure 7.2.

From the search result, I can touch the name of the boutique, which is high-lighted as a blue link. It takes me to the map view for that location. If I touch the phone number that's displayed in the result, it automatically dials the number. Or I can touch **Get Directions**, which opens a window such as the one shown in Figure 7.3. This enables me to choose whether to get the directions using Google Maps through the browser or through Maps on the device.

7

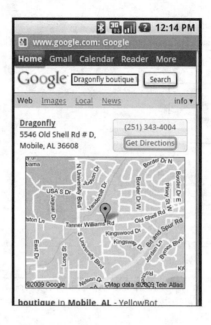

FIGURE 7.2

Search results appear differently on the Android phone, but you still have access to Google Maps data.

FIGURE 7.3

Choose whether to view the map through Google Maps in the Browser or Google Maps on the device. Viewing on the device gives you GPS capabilities as well.

Either option gets you the directions you seek. If you choose **Browser**, you move to the Google Maps page online that shows the map and opens the form for you to choose your starting location. Type in the address where you want to start at.

If you use the browser version of Google Maps, you have to enter more information. In addition, this version doesn't scale well: You need to scroll from left to right and top to bottom to access all the information. Using the browser version can be a frustrating exercise in not getting lost.

The other option, to get directions through the Google Maps application on your device, is a much better choice. This version is also much easier to use. When you touch the **Maps** option, the Maps application opens, as shown in Figure 7.4.

FIGURE 7.4
Touching the Maps option when you've selected Get Directions from a web search takes you to the Google Maps application on your device.

Where the map opens depends on whether you've used the map in the past and returned to your location when you finished the previous task. If you didn't close the map after your previous task, the first map that's shown when you open Maps is the last map you left it on. Don't worry—the map will change after you enter a starting address.

7

Type the starting address into the address field provided and touch the **Route** button. Alternatively, you can touch the small square to the right of the address field to open a menu of locations, as shown in Figure 7.5. The available locations include the following:

■ **My Current Location**—Uses your device's GPS capabilities to determine your current location. Directions then start from your current location.

■ **Contacts**—Opens a contacts file so you can select a starting address from those contacts. Only contacts for which you have added physical address appear in this list.

■ **History**—Opens a list of addresses that you've used to get directions in the past. If you have never used an address as a starting point, **My Current Location** is the only option that appears in this list.

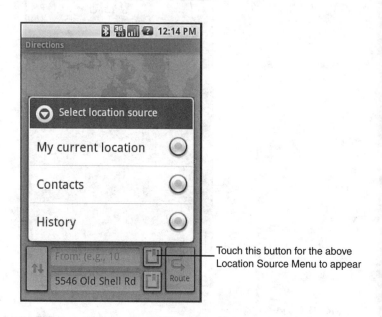

Touch this button for the above Location Source Menu to appear

FIGURE 7.5

Touch the square menu button to open a menu of location options. Use these options to create the starting address for directions.

This is the same method you would use for inputting an address if you opened the Maps application and wanted to get directions from a known address to a different known address. To do this without going through a search, open Maps and press the **Menu** key. Touch **Directions** from the menu that appears, and enter the **From** and **To** addresses in the address fields provided.

After you input a starting address and then touch the **Route** button, the application figures the most direct route from your starting location to the location that you wanted mapped (in this case, from the Google search that we did). Currently, the Android phone does not have real-time, turn-by-turn navigation, so the directions that are returned are as close as you'll get.

When these directions appear on your device (it could take a few seconds for the device to figure the correct directions and display them), you'll see the distance and the estimated drive time at the bottom of the screen. Two buttons also appear at the bottom of the screen: **Edit** and **Show Map**.

The **Edit** option takes you back to the previous screen, where you entered your starting location. From this screen, you can edit either the starting location or the destination.

The second option, **Show Map**, takes you to the map with the route that you requested mapped out. As shown in Figure 7.6, each point on the map has a marker on it, and a step-by-step capability is included. At each step in the directions, you can touch the arrow to the right of the directions box to go to the next step in the directions. The arrow to the left of the directions box takes you back to the previous step in the directions.

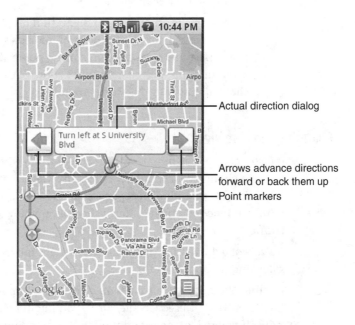

FIGURE 7.6

The Show Map option takes you to a map with the route mapped out and with markers at each step in the directions. You can navigate through these steps one direction at a time.

Additional Options

When you're in a map view, you can press the **Menu** key to open a menu of additional options:

- **Search**—Opens a search box at the top of the page that you can use to search for other locations anywhere in the world.

- **Directions**—Opens the address fields at the bottom of the screen so that you can change either the starting or ending address. You also can touch the **Route** button to open the written directions (instead of the map) to that location.

- **Clear Map**—Clears out the current map settings. This is useful if you've left the map set to directions from a previous trip and you want to clear out those directions.

- **My Location**—Takes the map back to your current location, based on a GPS reading.

- **Map Mode**—Enables you to switch among **Map**, **Satellite**, **Traffic**, and **Street View**. We've been working with **Map** view so far, but you'll learn more about the other three types of views in the next section, "Changing the Map View."

- **More**—Opens an additional menu that gives you access to three more commands. **History** opens a list of addresses that you've searched for in the past and used as your starting points. **Zoom** enables you to zoom in or out on the map that's shown. **About** opens a window that shows data about the Maps program.

Changing the Map View

You can change the map view that you're using when you're getting directions. To change your map view, press the **Menu** button from any map and then select **Map Mode**. This opens a menu similar to the one shown in Figure 7.7. To change map modes, touch the option you want: **Map**, **Satellite**, **Traffic**, or **Street View**.

We've worked with the **Map** option so far. It's a two-dimensional map, similar to looking at a paper map.

Satellite View shows you the map as a satellite image, as shown in Figure 7.8. If you've ever used Google Earth, you might be familiar with this view of maps. If you're looking for a little fun, try mapping your location using the Satellite view. See if you can pinpoint the time frame in which the satellite picture was taken. Those satellite images are rarely shown in real time.

7

FIGURE 7.7

The Map mode menu enables you to choose a Map View from the available options.

FIGURE 7.8

Satellite View shows you a satellite image of the map that you're working with.

In **Traffic View**, you should be able to see the feed from local traffic cameras. However, this works only on highways or interstate systems where traffic cameras are installed.

The last view available is **Street View**, one of the coolest features of the Android phone. Working with Maps and the GPS system, Street View can take you down to the street level so that you can see what an area might look like. It's great if you're looking for recognizable markers.

To enable Street View from within a map, press the **Menu** key and then touch **Map Mode**. Select **Street View** to go back to the map, but you'll start to see blue lines appear around the streets on the map. These lines indicate that cameras are available on those streets to give you a street view. Touch a street to see what camera is available nearest to where you touched, as shown in Figure 7.9.

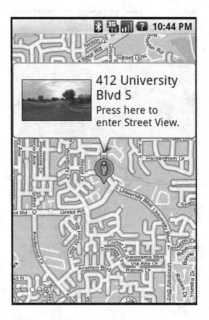

FIGURE 7.9

Touch the map while in Street View to show available cameras in the area you touched. When you find the one you want to view, touch it to open Street View.

When you find a camera near where you want to view at the street level on the map, touch that camera. The street view of the location opens on the device, as shown in Figure 7.10.

FIGURE 7.10

The Street View capabilities of the Android phone enable you to look at a location as if you're standing on the street, no matter where you're located.

While in Street View, you can also open a menu of additional options. This is the only screen on which these additional options appear. If you press the **Menu** key while in Street View, the following menu options appear (as shown in Figure 7.11):

- **Step Forward**—Moves the Street View image ahead by a few hundred yards
- **Step Backward**—Moves the Street View image backward by a few hundred yards
- **Zoom**—Opens the Zoom controls at the bottom of the screen so that you can zoom in or out on the image that's displayed
- **Go to Map**—Returns you to the two-dimensional map view
- **Report Image**—Opens a form in Google Maps on the Web where you can report an inappropriate image
- **Compass Mode**—Turns the compass mode on or off

FIGURE 7.11

Press the Menu key while in Street View to open an additional menu of options, including Compass Mode.

Street View's connection to the Android phone's Compass Mode is very cool. Touching Compass Mode enables and disables it, so pay attention to the confirmation message that you receive. When Compass Mode is enabled, the picture that you're looking at on the phone changes as you move around with your phone in Street View. For example, if you turn to the right or left, the image on the Android phone screen pans with you. Move the device up, and the image moves up; move it down and it follows. You can also use the trackball or finger movements on the screen to do the same thing.

However, Street View has one catch: It works only in areas that have webcams. For example, it works well in New York City because many webcams are present. It even works on the street we live on in Podunk, Alabama. However, it doesn't work on other streets in our city because no webcam exists to supply a street feed to the device.

Over time, more places will gain the webcam infrastructure that's needed for this feature to work everywhere. Until then, you might not find that it's always available—but when it is, it's very useful.

The Maps application on the Android-based phone is more than two-dimensional maps. It's not quite ready for real-time, turn-by-turn navigation, but that's just a matter of time. And until then, it's one of the best mapping capabilities in mobile phones.

Other GPS Capabilities

In addition to the mapping capabilities of the Android-based phone, other applications take advantage of the device's GPS capabilities. For example, third-party applications for weather enable you to find the current weather conditions and future weather forecasts based on GPS-provided location.

Other applications, such as GasBot, use your location (based on your GPS reading) to help you find the lowest gas prices near you. BreadCrumbz lets you create trail maps for places you travel to, using the GPS system to mark your location. You can upload photos and other information about that location so that others can see what's there or share your experiences in that particular spot.

Finally, an application called Follow Me enables you to register your device so that others can track it on the Web. You can use this application for social networking in the real world, or you can use it for things such as tracking your teenager's location so you know where he is at all times. This is the beginning of applications that take advantage of the GPS system on your Android-enabled phone. Over time, more applications will become available. When they do, they'll increase the richness of your interaction with the world.

Closing the Door

The GPS and mapping capabilities of the Android phone are probably one of the best features available on the device. These capabilities enable you to get directions, find places, track people, and share your traveling experiences. They help make the world a richer place. But as good as they are, they're not the only capabilities that you'll find useful on the Android phone.

For example, the next chapter is about the Android phone's entertainment features. Features such as music and YouTube make the Android phone more than just a tool—they make it fun, too. Keep reading to find out how.

7

Breaking Boredom with Entertainment Options

D riving the movement to handheld devices that are both phone and Internet capable is the desire to have a single device for communications, entertainment, and productivity needs. Before now, companies have struggled to reach that level of functionality.

With the latest round of mobile devices, including the T-Mobile Android phone and the iPhone, we're getting much closer to being able to use a single unit for everything. You've already seen how the Android phone can handle some of the basic functions of communication and productivity. But what about entertainment?

The Android phone has nailed down most aspects of entertainment. Rest assured that if you're caught in traffic or stuck waiting for an appointment, you'll have music, videos, games, and more to occupy your time when you're carrying the Android phone.

8

Listening to Music

Music makes the world go 'round.

That adage has been around for a while—probably as long as music. So it only makes sense for a device billed as a one-stop source for both communications and entertainment to have some type of music application.

The Android phone does have a music application. It's not an iTunes or Windows Media application, but it's still useful and very functional. It's also deceptively simple: Although the music application (shown in Figure 8.1) looks simplistic, it does a good job.

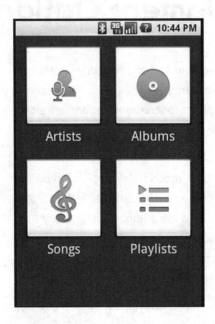

FIGURE 8.1

Although it looks simple, the Android phone's music application gives you good sound and access to music formats that aren't available on an iPod or iPhone.

The Android phone's music application is also more flexible than those available on other mobile devices and supports a variety of music formats, including these:

- AMR
- MIDI
- MP3
- M4A

- WMA
- WAV
- Ogg Vorbis

As you can see from this variety, you're not limited to a specific format. The G1's music player enables you to access any music format that is *DRM free*.

geek speak

DRM free means that the music is free of digital rights management (DRM) software. There are many companies now that sell DRM free music, and it can be downloaded in many places on the Internet.

Android also has a partnership with Amazon.com. Amazon provides Android-based phones with access to the Amazon MP3 marketplace. That means you can download songs directly from Amazon to your device for a low price. But we cover that in the "Putting Music on Your Device" section, later in the chapter. For now, let's look at how the music application works.

Finding Your Music

Using the music application is pretty straightforward, especially because it's more spartan than most—you won't get confused by controls that have no apparent bearing on listening to music.

To log onto the music application, select the **Music** icon from the applications menu. The screen that opens (called the library—you saw it in Figure 8.1) has icons for the four ways you can sort your music on the Android phone:

- **Artists**—Lists your music by artist, alphabetically
- **Albums**—Lists your music by albums, alphabetically
- **Songs**—Lists your music by songs, alphabetically
- **Playlists**—Lists your music by playlists, alphabetically

From the library, you can touch any one of the different icons to access your music, but you also have a search option if you want to quickly find the right song.

To reach the search option, press the **Menu** key. Two options appear: **Party Shuffle** and **Search**. Touch **Search** to open a list of all the songs on the device. Then start typing the name of the song you want (using the slide-out keyboard); the list narrows according to what you're searching for. You can also open any of the four methods of sorting music and begin typing to find what you're looking for.

Once you find a song that you want to listen to, touch the name of the song to open the music player (see Figure 8.2).

FIGURE 8.2

When you touch a song to play it, the player opens automatically and the song begins to play through your headphones or the built-in speaker on the device.

Using Music Controls

After you select a song to play, you'll see playback controls and information about the song displayed, including, if available, the name of the artist, the song, and the album, along with the album cover. A time display advances throughout the song so you can see how far into the song you are. Volume controls for the device speaker are located on the side of the unit, in the same place as your ring volume controls.

Buttons enable you to pause the music, skip forward to the next track, or skip back to the previous track. Three other buttons in the upper-right quadrant of the screen (see Figure 8.3) might not be immediately recognizable: **Playlist** takes you to the playlist display, **Shuffle** shuffles the playlist, and **Repeat** repeats the current song.

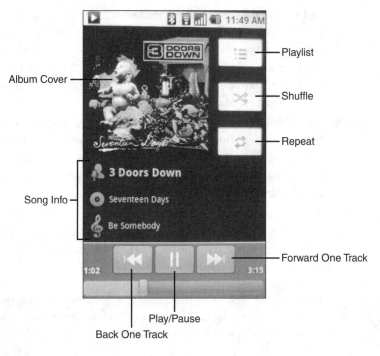

Album Cover

Song Info

Back One Track

Playlist

Shuffle

Repeat

Forward One Track

Play/Pause

FIGURE 8.3

The music player has a variety of onscreen controls.

As with nearly all the applications on the Android phone, the music player has another menu available when you press the **Menu** key. This menu contains the following options:

- **Library**—Takes you back to the main Library screen. The song that's playing when you touch the **Library** button continues to play, and the name and artist information displays at the bottom of the Library screen. Touch the artist's name to return to the song display.

- **Party Shuffle**—Shuffles the songs on your device, no matter what playlist they're on—think of it as a global shuffle option. If you're in the middle of a song when you touch this option, the song that's playing stops and a new song begins. Also, the Shuffle button changes to display a green globelike icon indicating that the Party Shuffle option has been activated.

- **Add to Playlist**—Opens a playlist menu. You can choose to add a song to the **Current Playlist**, a **New** playlist, or an existing playlist (but not the current one). If you touch **New**, a dialog box appears prompting you to enter a new playlist name with the keyboard. Alternatively, you can touch **Save** in the dialog box to give the playlist a default name, such as Exercise Music.

- **Use As Ringtone**—Sets the current song as the ringtone for your device. The next time you receive a call, the song will play in place of the ringtone you had previously set. Note that a song used as a ringtone only plays from the beginning of the track. There's no way to have it start with a song's chorus, for example.

- **Delete**—Deletes the song. Use this option carefully. When you delete a song, it's gone from the device permanently; if you don't have a copy on your computer, that means it's gone permanently.

Yellow Box

Some of these same controls are also available directly from the song title, artist, or album. A long touch on a song title opens a menu that gives you these options for a song: **Play**, **Add to Playlist**, **Use As Ringtone**, and **Delete**.

One last option for controlling your music is the window shade control. You're not forced to keep the music player open while your music is playing: You can move on to other things or simply return to the home screen. The music continues to play, and a music control appears in the notification area at the top of the screen.

When you're ready to change songs, turn off the music, or control it in any other way, pull down the window shade and touch the music control shown in Figure 8.4. That takes you back to the main song control screen that appeared when the music started playing.

Putting Music on Your Device

Now that you know how to control the music, you can learn how to add music to your device. You have three options: You can add music to the memory card, add music using a USB connection between your phone and a computer, or add music by downloading it from Amazon MP3. We cover the Amazon MP3 option in the next section. For now, let's look at the other two options.

FIGURE 8.4
Pull down the window shade notification area to reach background controls for your music; then touch the song name to open the full control screen.

Adding music to your phone by transferring it to the memory card requires you to have a computer with a memory card reader. If you do, simply plug in the memory card reader and then drag and drop your music files from their location on your computer to the **Music** folder on the memory card. After the files have transferred, insert the memory card back into the Android phone. Now you should have access to your music (assuming that it's in a recognized format).

If you don't have a card reader on your computer, you can still transfer music to your device using a USB connection between your computer and your device. Use these steps to transfer music to or from your device:

1. Connect your Android phone to your computer using the USB cable that was provided with the device. If this is the first time you've connected the device to the computer, it might go through a process of installing device drivers that tell your PC how to communicate with your phone. This should take only a few minutes.

2. When the drivers are installed, you should see a notification on the device that shows a USB icon in the notification area. If you pull down

the window shade to view the notification, you should see a message that reads, "USB connected. Select to copy file to/from your computer." Touch this message.

3. A notification pop-up appears asking if you want to mount your device to copy files between the device and the computer. Touch **Mount** to activate the connection between the two.

4. At this point, your computer's AutoPlay option should take over. When the AutoPlay window appears, select **Open Folder to View Files** to open your device as a portable hard drive on your computer, as shown in Figure 8.5.

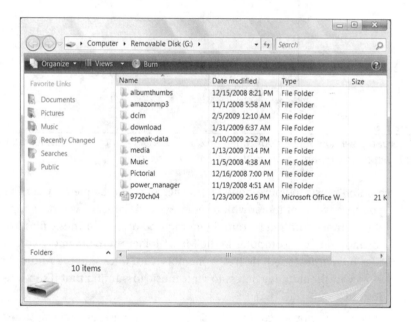

FIGURE 8.5
Select Open Folder to view files to open the Android phone as a portable device on your computer. Now you can transfer files between the computer and the Android phone.

5. Double-click the **Music** folder to open it.

6. On your computer, open a separate window to navigate to your **My Music** folder, or wherever you have your music files stored. You should now have two windows open, one for the computer and one for the device, as shown in Figure 8.6.

My Music folder

T-Mobile Android Phone
as a Portable Device

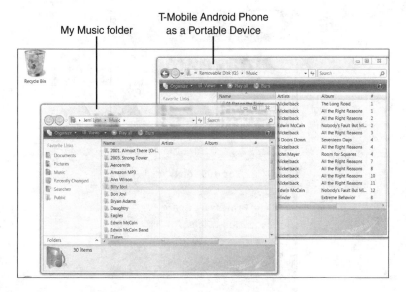

FIGURE 8.6

Drag and drop files from your computer to your device or from your device to your computer.

7. Drag files between windows to move them from the computer to the
device or from the device to the computer.

8. When you're finished, close both windows and disconnect the device
from the USB cable. Now you can find the music that you added to the
device in the music application.

Finding Music with Amazon MP3

The other way to add music to your device is with the Amazon MP3 application, which comes preinstalled on the Android phone. To reach it, go to the
applications menu and then touch the **Amazon MP3** icon.

The Amazon MP3 website, shown in Figure 8.7, appears. Here you can browse,
buy, and download DRM-free music.

You have several options to browse the music on Amazon. Buttons for **Top
100 Albums**, **Top 100 Songs**, **Browse by Genre**, and **Search** make it easy for
you to find the music you're looking for. As you're browsing, you can touch
the name of a song to play a short preview of it.

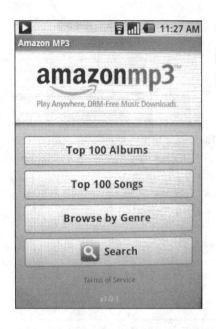

FIGURE 8.7

Use the Amazon MP3 site to browse, buy, and download music directly to your Android phone.

To purchase from Amazon MP3, you must have an Amazon account with a credit card or other payment method on file. When you find a song or album that you want to purchase, touch the **Buy** icon twice to go to a screen where you can log into your account.

After you've logged in, the purchase completes automatically and the download begins, as long as you're connected to a Wi-Fi network. Downloads won't complete over the wireless carrier's network, so if you make a purchase when you're not connected to a Wi-Fi network, the song will be queued but won't be downloaded until you have a Wi-Fi connection.

No Joke
Don't try to download music from the Amazon MP3 site as long as your device is connected to your computer via USB cable. Even if you're connected to a Wi-Fi, the download won't be able to complete as long as there's a USB connection between your device and a computer, because the memory card in the device is busy. If you're trying to download music and get an error that your SD card is full or unavailable, try disconnecting the device from the USB connection. That should free up the memory card to accept the download.

After you've purchased downloads from Amazon MP3, you can view those orders on the Amazon website. To see them, log into your account and click **My Account**. Next click **View Your Digital Orders** from the list beneath **Purchase History** to see a list of all your digital orders, including the downloads that you've purchased from your device. From this screen, you can select orders to print invoices and review purchases.

Amazon MP3 gives you a convenient option for purchasing digital music for your Android phone. And it's easy enough to use that you won't spend hours trying to figure everything out. In minutes, you can add your songs, download them, and be listening to your favorite music on your Android phone.

After you've added music directly to your device, however, you may want to transfer it to your computer. That's easy, too. All you have to do is connect the device to your computer, and then drag the music files from the **Music** folder on the device to your **My Music** folder on your computer. You can also listen to the music on your computer using your favorite music application.

Watching Videos with YouTube

Probably one of the hottest mobile applications right now is videos. From podcasts to music videos, everyone is watching videos on their mobile devices—or, at least, they *wish* they could watch videos on their mobile devices. With the Android phone, you can watch videos through the YouTube application.

As good as that sounds, the video applications with Android phone have limitations and playback of those videos you have recorded. The only video playback installed on the device is the YouTube application. If you want to download and view other videos such as television shows and movies, you have to find a third-party application at the Android Market that will give you those capabilities.

Those applications do exist, but some of them have strict requirements for what you can play; check carefully before you download one. One of the better video players is simply called Video Player by Jeff Hamilton. This application plays MPEG 4 files or 3GPP files with H.264 or H.263 protocols (these are just format protocols). It also plays MP3, AAC, and AMR audio files.

Accessing YouTube and Videos

You access YouTube as you do any other application. From the applications menu, touch the **YouTube** icon. The YouTube service opens to a page that lists some of the top-rated and most popular videos of the day. These are

8

constantly changing, so if you find something you like one time, it might not be there when you come back a second time.

Fortunately, you can search for what you want. Press the **Menu** key and then touch the **Search** option. This opens the search bar at the top of the page that you've seen in other applications.

Yellow Box

You don't have to go through the hassle of pressing the Menu key to reach a search option every time you want to search for something. On the slide-out keyboard of the G1 is a search button on the bottom line of buttons (on the myTouch, it's the magnifying glass button on the far right). This is a *contextual search button*—pressing it opens a search bar that's specific to whatever application you're using at the time. If you press this button while you're in YouTube, a search bar opens that lets you search the contents of YouTube for whatever video you want. You can try this handy feature in other applications, too.

Pressing the **Menu** key from that opening screen in YouTube offers other navigation options. In addition to having the **Search** option, you have **Favorites** (takes you to a list of the videos that you've marked as favorites), **Categories** (takes you to a list of video categories that you can browse), and **Settings** (opens a menu with one option—to clear your history).

Navigating a Video

When you find the video that you want to view, touch the title of the video; it loads and begins to play. Controls for the video briefly appear onscreen, as shown in Figure 8.8. These controls enable you to skip back or forward in the video and to pause the video or restart it after a pause. A yellow bar at the bottom of the screen shows the progress of the video and the time remaining.

These controls automatically hide if you don't access them for a few seconds. To make them reappear, touch the screen.

A set of controls also appears when you press the **Menu** key while a video is playing:

- **Favorite**—Adds a video to your favorites list.
- **Details**—Takes you to a page that displays information about the title and content of the video, as well as the number of views, its length, its publisher, the date added, and the permanent URL for the video. Below this information is a list of related videos.
- **Share**—Opens a Gmail message with the permanent URL for the video in the body of the message.

■ **Comments**—Opens a list of comments other YouTube visitors have made about the video.

■ **Home Page**—Returns you to the YouTube home page.

FIGURE 8.8

The onscreen controls enable you to pause or play a video or skip it forward or backward.

As time passes, new third-party applications might give you more options (such as recording video and uploading it to YouTube directly from your device), so check out the different video recording and playback options in the Android Market. Remember to check back often, too—developers are constantly updating the offerings at the Market.

Playing Games and Other Diversions

Currently, the Android phones come with no preinstalled games, but plenty are available on the Android Market.

You'll find dozens of third-party applications, such as Sudoku and BrainGenius, in four different categories of games: Arcade & Action, Brain & Puzzle, Cards & Casino (yes, Virginia, we have Solitaire), and Casual.

The variety of available games runs the gamut from fun and well designed to not-so-great. Many of the games are also limited-time trials, which means you might find one you really like, only to learn that you'll have to purchase the full version to have it available when you want it.

8

In addition to the games, you'll find Internet applications such as streaming video through ZooVision.

A radio application, such as Last.fm – Personal Radio, also gives you access to streaming radio over the Internet. So you'll have plenty to keep you occupied if you have some downtime. All you have to do is figure out which application you're most interested in.

Closing the Door

Videos, music, games, the Internet—all of these are almost as essential as a text-messaging service and a voice connection these days. Fortunately, the Android phones have the capabilities to keep you connected to the world in whatever form you find most comfortable.

Until now, we've talked a lot about adding applications from the Android Market. Now it's time to show you how to do add these apps. That's what's on tap for the next chapter. You'll be running all kinds of applications before you finish reading the text.

Adding Applications to Your Device

One of the biggest attractions of an Android-based phone is the availability of third-party applications for the phone. Third-party vendors can offer more useful applications than manufacturers can. For example, the Google applications that are built into the Android phones are great, but third-party developers can add usefulness to those apps by creating other apps that work with them.

Google was banking on this draw when it started the different developer challenges in the years preceding the release of the first Android phone, the G1. Google understands that people want a device that does more. With our busy lifestyles, we don't just want something that looks good and manages both our phone calls and out other communications messages—we want a device that proves itself useful as a tool.

Enter the Android Market. Google started to build on the Android Market with the first winners of the Mobile Developer Challenge. These were seed applications that first populated the Android Market and provided a foundation for what was to come.

IN THIS CHAPTER

■ Finding Apps in the Android Market

■ Downloading and Installing Apps

■ Managing Apps

From that time, hundreds of new applications have been added, with 5–10 new ones added daily. You'll find both free and fee-based apps on the Android Market. But even those that are fee-based are generally low cost. There are exceptions, of course, but for the most part, apps cost $3 to $10 each.

Regardless of the price of some apps, plenty are still free. What's more, because the Android Market is as open source as the Android development platform is, the apps that do appear in the Market will improve consistently. Every manner of app will be eventually be offered through the Android Market.

The Android Market and the related availability of open source applications there is perhaps one of the most important differentiators for the Android phone. Third-party applications aren't screened before they're released to the general population. Developers don't go through an approval process, and no corporate power rejects their applications. That means the variety of applications will be astounding, but it also means that numerous applications will be slight variations on the same function. For example, the Market has nearly a dozen To-Do applications, but many of them have one feature that's slightly more useful than others.

The sheer variety of applications that are currently available and that will be available in the future means that you might have to experiment a bit to figure out which ones work best for you.

Another disadvantage of the open nature of the Android Market is the possibility that some applications just aren't going to be of the highest possible quality. Developers push to get their apps on the market as soon as possible, sometimes at the expense of quality. At the time of this writing, there have been no malicious software files (like viruses or other malware) passed off as legitimate applications, but there have been lots of files that just don't perform well. So, how are you supposed to know which applications are worth downloading?

One of the best ways to determine how good or bad an application is on the Android Market is to look at the star ratings and reviews of the applications. Users can rate and review applications based on their experience with them. This isn't a foolproof method for determining how good or bad an application is, but it's usually helpful. It's also a reason that you should participate in the rate and review community at the Android Market. Share your constructive criticism as well as what you love about the applications you've tried to help other users determine which applications are right for them. You'll find more about using the rate and review process in the next section.

Finding Apps in the Android Market

So if hundreds of applications are available in the Android Market, how can you find the one that's right for you? As with most things Android, you have choices. You can find an app in more than one way, just as there are so many different types of apps available.

The most general method of finding applications in the Android Market is to simply browse. You can browse applications in several ways:

1. From the applications menu, select the **Android Market** icon.

2. You're taken to the Android Market (see Figure 9.1). From here, you can select **Applications**, **Games**, **Search**, or **My Downloads**.

FIGURE 9.1

At the Android Market, you'll find both games and productivity applications for your Android-based device.

3. Select **Applications** to go to a list of the different categories of applications. These categories range from Communications and Entertainment to Reference and Shopping.

4. Select **Games** to see a list of game categories that includes Arcade & Action, Brain & Puzzle, Cards & Casino, and Casual.

9

5. Select **Search** to open a search window. Then type in the name of the application you're trying to find.

6. Browse the available applications in the subcategory of search results until you find an application that interests you. You can touch the title of any application to move to an information page, such as the one shown in Figure 9.2, where you'll find a description of the application along with user ratings and feedback for the application. Download buttons also appear on this page, but we come back to those in the next section.

FIGURE 9.2

Tap the title of any application or game to learn more about it and to see how other Android users rate it.

As you're browsing the applications, you'll also notice two tabs at the top of the application listings page, as shown in Figure 9.3. This enables you to further sort the applications **By Popularity** and **By Date**.

When you sort applications by popularity, the applications with the most stars appear at the top of the list, progressing down to the applications with the fewest stars. You can join in by rating these applications, too.

Sorting Tabs

FIGURE 9.3

Sort applications by popularity or date.

Back on the main Android Market page is one additional option that we haven't talked about yet. **My Downloads** takes you to a list of the applications that you've downloaded and that are still installed on your device. If you've downloaded applications and deleted them from the device, they won't show up in this list anymore. (If you want to leave a comment about an application or rate it, do so before you uninstall the app.)

To rate or comment on the apps in your downloaded list, follow these steps:

1. Touch the title of the application that you want to rate or comment on. This opens an information page similar to the one shown in Figure 9.4.

2. To add a star rating, touch the stars next to **My Rating**. This opens a Rate It window, as shown in Figure 9.5.

3. Touch the number of stars that you want to give the application. Then touch **OK** to save the rating and return to the information page. You can also touch **Cancel** if you change your mind and decide not to rate the application.

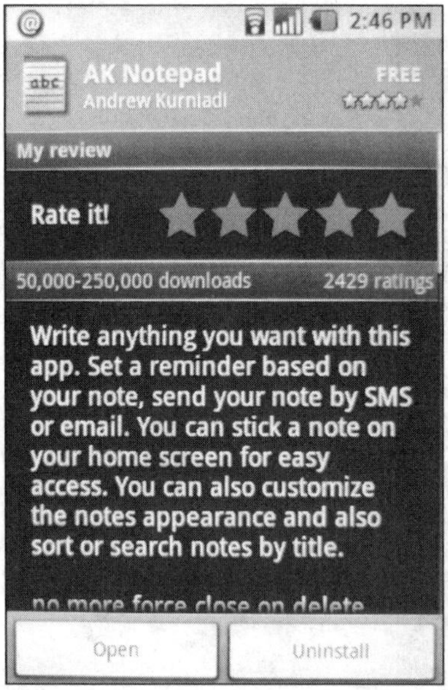

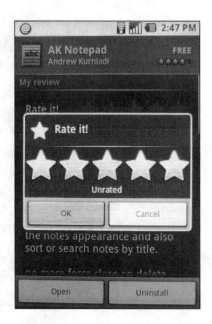

FIGURE 9.4

On the information page, you can rate and review applications, but you'll also see information about the application and the number of downloads and ratings.

FIGURE 9.5

Choose the number of stars you want to give an application, from one (worst) to five (best).

4. Back on the information page, a **Post a Comment** link appears directly beneath the star rating. Touch this to open a dialog box where you can type your comment (see Figure 9.6).

5. After you've entered your comment, touch the **OK** button to save the comment. If you change your mind, you can always touch **Cancel** to return to the information page without leaving a comment.

6. When you're finished rating and reviewing the application, you can press the Home button to return to the Home screen. Your ratings and review are automatically saved to an online server so other Android Market users can see them.

FIGURE 9.6

Type the comment you want to appear in the Android Market for the application you've downloaded.

When reviewing applications, you can clear your review at any time. Most applications are changed or updated frequently, and these changes or updates can affect the way you feel about an application. If you want to change your review, follow these steps:

1. Open the information page for an application that you previously reviewed.

2. Press the **Menu** key to open a menu of additional options.

3. Touch **More** on the menu. This opens another menu, with two more options.

4. Select **Clear My Review** to remove both the star rating that you assigned the application and the comments you made.

You might have noticed additional options when you opened the menu from the information page. Those options are pretty self-explanatory, but you might want to know more about two: **Security Permissions** and **Flag Content**.

The **Security Permissions** option takes you to a page that explains what other applications and information the application has access to (see Figure 9.7). Most applications work with other applications, with your personal information, or perhaps even with the hardware controls on the device. This list tells you exactly what other access the application has.

FIGURE 9.7

Most applications work with other applications, data, or hardware on your device. This screen lists the partnerships the application makes with those other resources.

The second option, **Flag Content**, is an option that enables you to flag objectionable content. When you choose this option, a new screen, similar to the one shown in Figure 9.8, appears. Four options are available.

Although Android Market is an open marketplace, developers are required to adhere to certain guidelines. You can find these guidelines at www.google.com/mobile/android/market-policies.html.

If you find that an application doesn't meet these guidelines and want to report it as objectionable, touch the appropriate option and then touch **Submit**. The report is filed with the Android Market, and the application is reviewed. However, the folks at Android aren't promising that they'll remove the application—they promise only to "take action if appropriate."

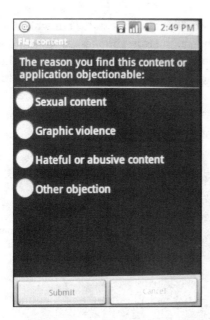

FIGURE 9.8

If you find applications that contain objectionable content or that don't adhere to Android guidelines, you can submit them for review.

Downloading and Installing Apps

With so many applications to choose from, you'll probably want to install plenty of them. Installation is a simple process. When you're reviewing the information about the application, you'll see an **Install** button at the bottom of the screen (see Figure 9.2): Touch the button to install the app.

A new page appears that shows you the list of information and resources the application requires access to. If you touch the **Show All** button on the screen, you open a list of additional resources that are used (if there are additional resources). Review the list; if you agree to allow the application access to those resources, touch **OK**.

Now all you have to do is wait. The length of time it takes to download and install the application varies by the application's size and by the speed of the network you're connected to. Most download and installation processes don't last more than three to five minutes, and the whole process takes place in the background.

A download icon shows in your status bar while the application is loading. When it's complete, the icon changes, as shown in Figure 9.9. To access the application, pull down the notifications window shade and touch the notification. The new application opens and you can begin using it immediately.

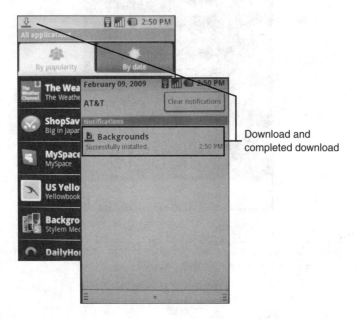

FIGURE 9.9

Applications download and install in the background. When finished, a notification appears in the status bar that you can use to access the app for the first time.

That's all there is to installing applications from the Android Market. The glory of the Android-based device is that it handles everything else for you. Applications automatically install to the memory card, and after you allow permissions for the resource sharing, you're done until it's time to play with your new toy. Pretty impressive, huh?

Managing Apps

If you're like us, you'll find a lot of applications that sound cool but that you won't use often or that, after you get them on your device, aren't quite what you thought they were. Not a problem. Managing the applications on your Android-based device is a lot easier than managing applications on a computer.

Even updating an application that you've downloaded from the Market is taken care of for you. The first time you access an application after an update becomes available, you'll receive a notice that the app needs to be updated. Touch **Update Now** to enable the update. You also must touch **Install** when the installation screen appears, but then, as with the original download, the installation takes on its own life.

Removing Apps the Easy Way

Removing unwanted applications is easy, too. The hardest part is figuring out which of the two ways to remove applications you want to use. The easiest way is to follow these steps:

1. Enter the Android Market by selecting the **Android Market** icon from the applications menu.

2. Touch **My Downloads** on the main Android Market screen.

3. Select the application that you want to remove from the list of installed applications.

4. On the screen that appears, touch the **Uninstall** button. A confirmation message similar to the one shown in Figure 9.10 appears.

FIGURE 9.10

Before an application is deleted, you'll receive a confirmation message, just to be sure you intended to remove it from the device.

5. Touch **OK** to complete the uninstallation. If you change your mind, and decide not to uninstall the application, you can touch **Cancel** to return to the previous screen.

No Joke Be careful about removing applications from your device. After you touch **OK** on the confirmation screen, there's no way to undo the removal of the app. You can download and reinstall the application, but if you had any data stored in the application, it will be gone for good.

Managing Apps, Including Removal

You can manage and remove applications in a more involved process as well.

To further manage your applications, start from the Home screen. Press the **Menu** key and then select **Settings** from the menu that appears. On the settings screen, touch **Applications**. You're taken to the **Application Settings** page. From this page, you can manage how applications from unknown sources are downloaded. Place a check mark in the box to allow applications from unknown sources; deselect the option to disallow it.

We recommend keeping this option deselected unless you know that you'll need it. Applications from unknown sources can potentially harm your device.

Quick Launch

The next option on **Application Settings** is **Quick Launch** (see Figure 9.11). This option enables you to assign a keyboard combination to an application so that you can launch it from the keyboard without having to navigate back to the Home screen or the Apps menu.

To assign a keyboard combination to an application, follow these steps:

1. On the **Quick Launch** screen, touch a letter that has **Assign Application** in blue.

2. A list of available applications appears. Touch the application you want to assign a keyboard combination to.

3. The **Quick Launch** screen appears again, but this time, the letter that you chose has the application name and the keyboard combination to access it, as shown in Figure 9.12.

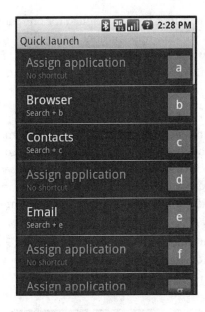

FIGURE 9.11

The Quick Launch page enables you to see keyboard shortcuts and assign shortcuts to applications.

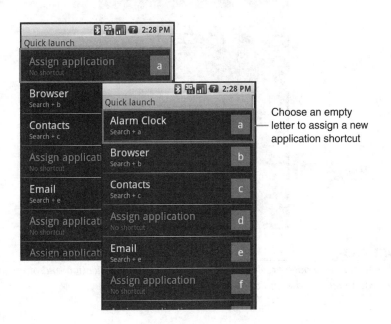

Choose an empty letter to assign a new application shortcut

FIGURE 9.12

Use available Quick Launch letters to assign keyboard shortcuts to your favorite applications.

To clear a shortcut that you've assigned (or one that's preassigned), long-touch the shortcut. A window appears confirming that you want to clear the shortcut. Touch **OK** to clear it and return to the Quick Launch window, or touch **Cancel** to return to the Quick Launch window without clearing the shortcut.

Manage Applications

The next option on the **Application Settings** menu is **Manage Applications**. Here you find another option for removing applications from the device. When you touch this option, it might take a few seconds for the applications screen to appear. This is because the system is examining the applications that are installed on your device and computing the space required for them.

When the screen appears, touch the application you want to manage. An **Application Info** page appears (shown in Figure 9.13) that tells you the amount of storage the application uses; it also shows the default options for the application and the permissions that application enables.

FIGURE 9.13

The Application Info page provides information about the application and offers an additional way for you to remove the app or manage its defaults.

You can uninstall an application from the Application Info screen as well. Touch the **Uninstall** button and then touch **OK** on the confirmation page.

No Joke One thing you should know about paid applications is that there is currently no default method for backing them up, so if you uninstall an application that you paid for, you may have to repurchase it before you can re-install it. An alternative is to purchase one of the backup programs, like MyBackup Pro, from the Android Market and create a backup of all of your paid applications.

Some applications also have **Defaults** set. Defaults are the default settings for how an application manages other applications or settings. You can clear these defaults by touching the **Clear Defaults** button.

Development Settings

The last option on the **Application Settings** menu is **Development**. This menu has only two options: **USB Debugging** and **Stay Awake**.

The **USB Debugging** option enables you to put the device in debug mode when it's connected to a computer via a USB connection. This allows developers and programmers to debug the applications that they've created. Unless you are a developer or programmer, you probably won't need this option.

The other option is **Stay Awake**. This sets your system to never go into sleep mode while it's charging. For a developer or programmer, this is helpful in keeping the device active during long periods of coding. But even if you're not a programmer or coder, you might find the option useful for keeping the device awake while it's charging. This is especially useful if you have a background or pictures on your home screen that you want to be able to view while the device is charging.

Closing the Door

The Android Market is a great resource for your Android-based device. The open nature of the Market enables developers and programmers to create applications not only that are truly useful, but also that can be updated and improved continually.

Finding and installing the applications is simple, too. Even managing all your applications is point-and-click. But what if you want to create apps? If you have computer programming experience, you can do that, too. Creating apps requires some knowledge of a programming language such as Java, but beyond that, working with Android-based applications is easier than programming from scratch.

You'll learn all about this in the next part of the book. Upcoming chapters walk you through understanding Android and the Android SDK, and provide instructions to help you develop your first Android apps.

9

The Android Platform

In this part:

- Getting to Know Android
- Developing Native Android Apps
- Developing Mobile Web Applications
- Advanced Android Apps

If playing with the applications available for the Android platform is half the fun of owning an Android device, then developing those apps is the other half. In Part III, we show you how to get started developing applications for Android.

Chapter 10, "Getting to Know Android," is your true introduction to the Android stack. Up to this point, you've seen some of the basics of Android, but if you really want to get to know Android, this is the place you'll find all the information you're looking for.

We really dig into the development part of Android in Chapter 11, "Developing Native Android Apps." This is where you'll find the basic design principles that you need to know for developing any mobile application. It's not Android just yet, but read this chapter—you need this information to create great Android apps.

Chapter 12, "Developing Mobile Web Applications," is where you really get into Android applications. In this chapter, you'll learn what tools you need to start developing applications, as well as how to install and use those tools.

Chapter 13, "Advanced Android Apps," finally gets into building applications. You'll learn how to build basic applications and how to publish them on the Android Market for other people to enjoy.

If creating applications is your thing, you'll find everything you need to know to get started with Android right here. So why wait? A whole world of people out there are waiting on your application. Learn how to create it in these pages.

Getting to Know Android

In previous chapters, you learned that Android is a technology stack for mobile devices. It includes a Linux kernel–based operating system, middleware, and many key applications. In this chapter, you'll gain a better understanding of the Android platform and how the Open Handset Alliance guides its development.

Understanding Android

Android is not just a software development platform for mobile devices or a framework for developing applications. It differs from other mobile development technologies such as Java Micro Edition and the .NET Compact Framework. It's built from the bottom up as a *stack* of capabilities. The Linux kernel operating system is at the bottom of the stack, controlling the drivers and hardware management. The next level houses the libraries that applications draw on, including the core libraries for Android.

geek speak   *Stack* refers to a layer of components that make the Android platform, helping you understand how different Android components are glued together.

Above that layer is the application framework, where the applications that you interact with do all their work. The final layer in the stack, the one that the user sees, is a set of key applications that are shipped along with the device or that you can install on the device from third-party developers. Figure 10.1 shows a graphical representation of the Android stack.

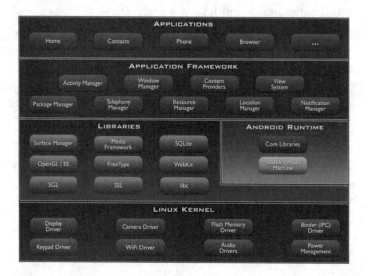

FIGURE 10.1

The Android architecture is different than other mobile platforms; it's built specifically to make the best use of available resources.

Key Components of Android

Android is designed to be different from other mobile platforms. As you've already learned, Android makes the best use of available resources by sharing those resources. But this doesn't just happen. The whole platform is designed so that sharable resources are available through the use of stacking.

In the stacking method used to develop the Android platform, resources that are devoted specifically to the device reside at the bottom of the stack. Each progressive level above that becomes more sharable. Let's take a closer look at each level of the stack:

■ **Linux kernel**—The base of the Android stack is the Linux kernel. The Android Linux kernel is based on Linux Version 2.6. This kernel acts as the layer between the mobile-device hardware and the rest of the Android stack. It manages memory, processes, file systems, and all I/O operations.

Linux is a popular operating system that comes in many different flavors, built on top of the freely distributed Linux system kernel. Similar to an operating system on a computer providing an interface to the hardware, the Linux kernel in Android acts as an interface to your mobile devices.

■ **Android runtime**—On top of the Linux kernel is the *Android runtime*. Android includes a *virtual machine* called Dalvik that runs Java applications and is optimized for mobile devices to run with a low memory footprint and optimized hardware resource. Every Android application runs in its own process within a Dalvik virtual machine. The application is packaged into a Dalvik executable file that the Dalvik virtual machine executes.

geek speak

A virtual machine is an environment on top of which your programs are executed. A virtual machine provides services such as memory management to executing programs. All compiled Java programs run on a byte-code interpreter, the Java Virtual Machine or JVM. Dalvik is the Android JVM.

The Android runtime is an environment (which includes the Dalvik virtual machine) for executing your Android applications.

The Android runtime also contains a set of core libraries that provide different functionality. You can access these functions when you're creating your own custom Android applications.

Core libraries are libraries that expose functions of a system. Referencing core libraries enables you to use the functions in your applications.

■ **Libraries**—The Android stack includes two sets of libraries. One set is core libraries that provide different functionality to the applications that run on Android. You can access these functions when creating your custom Android applications. These libraries help you include functionality in your applications that someone else has already created. This reduces the time spent on developing applications and can increase functionality because other developers continually improve the libraries.

The second set of libraries in the Android stack are native libraries developed using the C and C++ languages. This set includes support for different types of 2D and 3D media, a lightweight database, and so on. You do not access these libraries directly in your applications.

■ **Application Framework**—The C and C++ libraries in the Android stack are exposed to developers and other applications through the *Application Framework*. The Application Framework also enables applications to register functionality that the other applications can reuse.

The Application Framework provides a common set of core services that all applications can share. This includes services such as an activity manager to manage the life cycle of Android applications, a resource manager to manage application resources such as strings and images, and other services.

Application Framework is a common framework for developing your applications. It enables you to use many features that the Application Framework already provides, instead of having to start every application from scratch.

■ **Applications**—The Android stack ships with a basic set of applications. This includes an email client, short message service (SMS) client, calendar, browser, and contacts application. Part 2, "The Applications," covered these applications. If you skipped that part of the book, you can flip back at any time to learn more about how they work. Any custom application that you create also lives along with other applications in this part of the Android stack.

Features of the Android Platform

Android has some distinct features that make it stand out from the rest of mobile technologies. Let's look at some of those special features.

- **Open platform**—Android is an open source project. The Open Handset Alliance enables development of the Android platform, with each member committed to the openness of the mobile platform. This encourages a variety of input and different views on Android's development. As an application developer, you can thus understand the platform better.

- **Easy access to core features**—Android includes a rich set of libraries to access all the core mobile features within your custom Android applications. The Application Framework stack of the Android platform enables you to access these features through Java class libraries. For example, to send an SMS programmatically, you can reference the necessary libraries and execute the method that sends the SMS. You don't need to know the internals on how the SMS is sent.

- **Extendable and replaceable applications**—You can extend Android applications, including the core applications shipped with your mobile device, to provide new innovative features. Going one step further, you can even replace any of the core Android applications with a custom application that you create. For example, you can create your own application to manage contacts and designate that application as the default application for managing contacts.

- **Borderless applications**—Android applications are borderless and not confined to a single executable. Android applications use core features available in the mobile device. They also can communicate with other custom Android applications, exposing features for other applications to use.

  For example, you might create an application that provides certain data about geographic locations. Another application might use that information to provide the best holiday destinations. The applications are not restricted and can keep growing in new functionalities.

- **Web friendly**—Google, one of the key members of the Open Handset Alliance, plays an important part in the development of the Android platform. Therefore, you can expect the Android platform to work seamlessly with the Web. Android applications can render web content by embedding HTML and JavaScript.

10

10

IS GOOGLE TAKING OVER THE (MOBILE) WORLD?

Google is a key player in developing the Android SDK. As you might recall from Chapter 1, "The Theory of the Android Phone," Google invested heavily in the development of Android. However, concerns surfaced that Google might dominate the development process, and that other organizations might be locked into creating Android innovations as Google dictated.

Fortunately, Google seems to be giving developers the freedom they need to develop the applications they want to develop. Unlike the Apple Marketplace for iPhone and iPods, Google isn't censoring the applications that are developed, beyond ensuring that applications are not harmful or offensive to users.

Google also helped start an alliance of other companies, developers, and organizations interested in the value of an open-mobile platform. With luck, the Open Handset Alliance will help reassure people that although Google is a guiding force for Android, it isn't a dictatorship.

One thing is certain: The landscape of mobile development is changing. What will come from these changes remains to be seen. However, it's almost certain that the changes will be good, and the result will be a better mobile experience for all users.

The Principles of the Open Handset Alliance

Even though Google is the company that comes to mind when you think of Android, it isn't the only company involved in developing the Android platform. Many other players are involved in Android, and each of those players brings something special to the table. Each has a core set of capabilities to offer and wants to see the openness of the Android platform work.

The Open Handset Alliance

The Open Handset Alliance is a group of technology companies creating innovation around the Android platform. At press time, 47 companies formed the Open Handset Alliance. The primary goal of these companies is to develop open standards for mobile devices.

The Open Handset Alliance includes some large organizations that are leaders in various aspects of mobile technologies, including Google, Vodafone, Intel, Motorola, and Toshiba, to name a few. The members of the Open Handset Alliance are committed to the commercial success of the Android platform.

The members of the Open Handset Alliance fall into one of the following categorization groups:

- **Mobile operators**—Mobile operators are companies that provide mobile subscriptions through a mobile network. The Android platform enables mobile operators to customize their services and provide handsets at lower costs. The flexibility of the Android platform also enables them to differentiate their lines of services from those of their competitors. Some of the key mobile operator members in the Open Handset Alliance are T-Mobile and Sprint Nextel.

- **Software-development companies**—The openness of the Android platform enables software companies to create innovative applications. This also extends the capabilities of the mobile device by creating new applications for the Android handset, such as different types of business and game applications. Some key members from this category are Google and eBay.

- **Semiconductor companies**—Semiconductor companies or chip manufacturers play a vital part in creating processors to power the mobile devices. The participation of these companies allows the android platform to take advantage of innovations in the mobile devices. Some key members from this category are Broadcom and Intel.

- **Commercialization companies**—Commercialization companies promote and ensure the commercial success of the Android platform. Some key members from this category are Aplix and Noser Engineering.

- **Handset providers**—Handset providers benefit from the Android platform by creating handsets that have lower software costs. The extensible and replaceable nature of the Android platform also enables handset providers to ship the handsets with different applications, thereby differentiating their products from their competitors'. Some key members from this category are HTC and Motorola.

Alliance versus Single Provider

One of Android's important strengths is that it's backed by different companies that are part of the Open Handset Alliance. The success of a mobile
phone depends on a wide range of companies, ranging from the handset
manufacturers to the mobile application developers. Having members that
span different areas encourages more innovation than a single vendor could
provide.

Closing The Door

Android is open and very usable. Google won't likely dominate Android or
dictate to members of the Open Handset Alliance how the platform should
develop. The platform truly is open and useful.

Now that you understand more about the Android stack of technology and
how the different levels of the stack work together to create a mobile platform
that's both useful and extensible, it's time to move on to developing content
for Android.

In Chapter 11, "Developing Native Android Apps," we look at the principles
of developing mobile web applications, from designing web content for the
Android-based device to creating mobile content that performs well on the
device. Before you know it, you'll be creating Android applications and
uploading them to the Android Market.

Developing Native Android Apps

You know all the features of an Android handset and have started playing with it. You have an idea for a brilliant application that you wish was shipped with the Android handset. You decide to create the application yourself and experience the excitement of running your application on your Android handset.

In this chapter, we take a look at developing native Android applications. Native Android applications are applications that run within the Android runtime on an Android handset. Let's look at what you need to get started developing native Android applications.

Requirements for Development

Before you write your first Android application, you must set up an environment for building your Android application. This section introduces you to a few prerequisites.

Android Software Development Kit (SDK)

The Android SDK is a set of tools and libraries for creating native Android applications. The Android SDK also includes an emulator that enables you to test your Android application before deploying it to an actual Android handset. You can download the Android SDK from http://code.google.com/Android/download.html.

geek speak A Software Development Kit (SDK) is a set of tools and libraries for creating applications. Typically, a vendor of a product releases an SDK to provide programmable access to the product functionalities.

Java Standard Edition Development Kit (JDK)

The JDK contains tools and libraries for you to create applications that run on the Java Virtual Machine. The Java programming language is used in developing applications that use the JDK. Java is a C-like object-oriented programming language and supports many features, including the capability to run applications created on multiple platforms. You can download the JDK from http://java.sun.com/javase/downloads/index.jsp

Eclipse Integrated Development Environment (IDE)

Eclipse is an IDE for developing applications. It is a preferred development platform for creating applications on many platforms such as JDK and Aptana. You can use Eclipse to develop desktop and mobile applications using the JDK integration. It's an open source application that IBM originally developed. It has a good plug-in model that easily integrates other tools. Although this isn't required when creating Android applications, using an IDE simplifies your development process by providing easy access to most of the tools available in the Android SDK. An IDE also provides syntax highlighting, code completion, running and debugging environments for testing your application, and other useful features. You can download the Eclipse IDE from http://www.eclipse.org/downloads/www.eclipse.org/downloads/. (From this point on, we assume you are using version 3.4 of Eclipse, also known as "Ganymede.")

An Integrated Development Environment (IDE) is a development environment that provides easy access to tools used during application development. At minimum, an IDE includes an editor (to write code) and a compiler (to compile code). It can also contain debuggers, testing tools, and access to version-control tools.

ANT Build Tool

ANT (Another Neat Tool) is a build tool frequently used for building Java applications. ANT is an open source project maintained by Apache. It enables you to define a XML file listing a set of tasks that can be performed. You can invoke the tasks defined in this build file by using the command-line tool ANT. Common tasks that build tools like ANT do include creating directories, files, running language compilers, and even cleaning up any temporary files generated during "the build." You can download the latest version of ANT from http://ant.apache.org/.

Build tools enable you to automate a build process by automatically executing a list of tasks that must happen to build an application. These tasks can invoke different tools to compile code, package, and deploy your application.

Developing Android Applications

Now that you know the prerequisite software required for creating your own Android applications, you'll get your hands dirty by setting up a development environment and creating your first application. Remember, this section helps you understand how all these tools work together, not to understand what the code does. Let's build a basic Android application to help you understand what these tools do.

Setting Up the Development Environment on Windows

In this section, you'll configure the tools to create your first Android application on the Windows platform. If you're not a Windows user, skip to the next section, which explains how to configure the tools for a Linux distribution. Even though the steps describe configuring the environment on the Windows Vista platform, they are identical for other releases of the Windows operating system.

1. Download and install the Java Standard Edition Development Kit. This installs the complete set of tools and libraries for developing Java applications. Make sure the version that you install is either JDK 5 or a later version (JDK 6 preferred).

2. Download the ANT binaries. Unzip the zip file using your favorite utility.

3. Download the Android SDK. Unzip the zip file using your preferred zip utility.

4. To ensure that you can run the command-line tools from JDK, ANT, and Android, it is convenient to set some environment variables within Windows. This ensures that you can run the tools from any directory. Setting these variables also helps these tools find each other. For example, ANT relies on JDK, so setting the necessary environment variables will help ANT find the path to the JDK tools.

To set these variables, go to the **Control Panel**, select **System and Maintenance**, and then select **System**. In the System window, select **Advanced System Settings** and select **Environment Variables** (see Figure 11.1). Create the user variables ANDROID_HOME, JAVA_HOME, and ANT_HOME to point to the respective directories where you have extracted or installed Android, JDK, and ANT. Next, create a PATH user variable and set the value to %PATH%;%JAVA_HOME%\bin;%ANDROID_HOME%\tools;%ANT_HOME%\bin. This enables you to access the command-line tools from any location.

No Joke   Environment variables contain variables that many applications installed in your system might share. Make sure you don't delete any existing environment variables, because other programs might depend on them. Also make sure that you set only the user variables, not the system variables. User variables are settings for the current logged in user and the system variables are settings for all users of the system. Although setting these variables as system variables makes them available for all users in your system, it increases the chances of mistakenly changing something that other programs use.

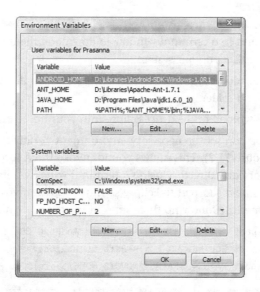

FIGURE 11.1
Setting environment variables.

5. To ensure that you have set the environment variables correctly, open a command prompt and try the commands `javac`, `ant`, and `adb`. If you have set everything correctly, you should get usage information on how to use those commands. If you get an error with the message that the command is not recognized as an internal or external command, you must revisit the created variables and make sure that you have set the information correctly.

6. Download Eclipse. Unzip the zip file using your preferred zip utility. If required, create a shortcut to your desktop for `eclipse.exe` to invoke Eclipse easily.

Setting Up the Development Environment on Linux

Not a lot of difference arises when configuring the environment on the Linux platform. The following steps explain how to configure the development environment on Ubuntu Linux:

1. Download and install the Java Standard Edition Development Kit. Use the `sudo apt-get install sun-java6-jdk` command in a terminal window to download and install JDK 6 on your system.

11

2. Download and install ANT. Use the `sudo apt-get install ant` command in a terminal window to download the necessary software and install it on your system.

3. Download the Android SDK compressed zip file. Unzip Android SDK into a folder.

4. Download and extract Eclipse into your home directory.

5. You can set the necessary environment variables in the .bashrc file (see Figure 11.2). This allows you to invoke the Android tools and Eclipse from any directory using a terminal window. Alternatively, you can create a shortcut to Eclipse so that you can invoke it from your desktop. Enter the following three lines in your `.bashrc` file:

```
export ANDROID_HOME = <<Path to Android SDK folder>>
export ECLIPSE_HOME = <<Path to eclipse>>
export PATH = $PATH:$ANDROID_HOME/tools:$ECLIPSE_HOME
```

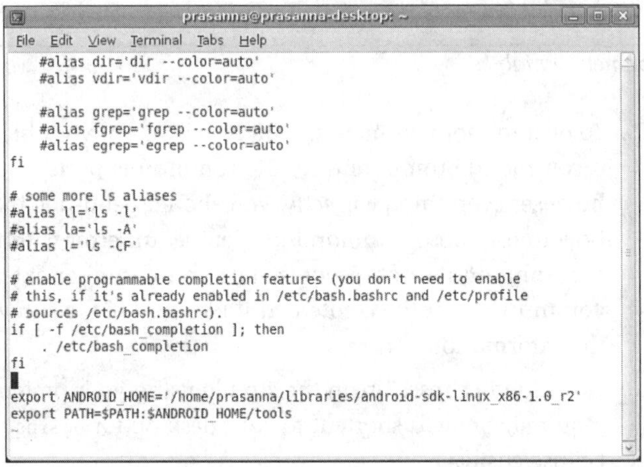

FIGURE 11.2
Setting environment variables in `.bashrc`*.*

6. Now you can invoke Eclipse by typing `eclipse` in the terminal window. Similarly, you can invoke the other Android tools directly from the terminal window as well.

Making your IDE Android Aware

By default, Eclipse does not support the creation of Android applications. To create Android applications, you must download and install the Android

Development Tools (ADT) plug-in. This makes the necessary project templates available and grants access to Android tools right from Eclipse.

You can install ADT by configuring Eclipse to update and manage ADT as an add-on.

1. Open Eclipse and click the **Help** menu option; then click **Software Updates**.

2. Select the **Available Software** tab.

3. Click **Add Site** and enter **http://dl-ssl.google.com/Android/eclipse** as the location; then click **OK**. This shows the available packages (see Figure 11.3).

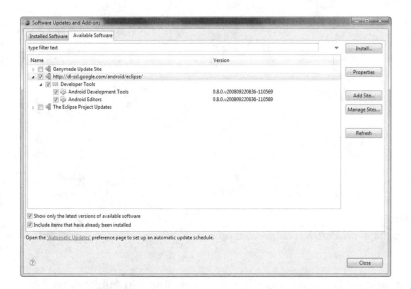

FIGURE 11.3

ADT packages available for Eclipse.

4. Select both **Android Editors** and **Android Development Tools**, click **Install**, and click **Finish**. This installs the necessary plug-ins in Eclipse so that you can create Android applications and work with the Android SDK tools from Eclipse.

If you cannot connect to the remote site and use the software update feature of Eclipse, you can opt for a manual download of ADT. Download the ADT zip file from http://code.google.com/Android/adt_download.html. In the Add Site dialog, instead of entering the URL as the location, click **Archive**. Then browse and select the downloaded ADT zip file.

The final step in configuring Eclipse is to let Eclipse know the location of the Android SDK. In Eclipse, click the **Windows** menu option and then click **Preferences**. Select **Android** and set the **SDK Location** to the directory where you have extracted the Android SDK, as shown in Figure 11.4. You can also set additional preferences, such as options for the emulator and logging levels, if required.

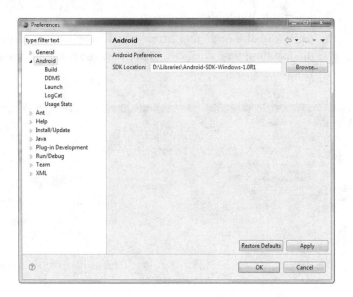

FIGURE 11.4
Setting the Android SDK Location in Eclipse.

Bringing It All Together: Creating Your First Android Application

There are two ways to create an Android application using the tools we've discussed thus far. One is to create the application by issuing commands in a terminal or command window, another is to create the application from within the IDE, Eclipse. This section discusses creating the application using both methods. First, from the command window and then from Eclipse.

To create a project, use the android script (found in the android/tools directory). Open a command prompt and run this command:

```
android create project -a HelloAndroidGeek -k .
    ➥com.samples.HelloAndroidGeek -t 2 -p
/home/<username>/AndroidProjects/HelloAndroidGeek
```

The complex android script is used for creating many Android-related items, including new projects (as shown here) and Android virtual devices. The "-a HelloAndroidGeek" specifies the name of the derived activity class for the project. The "-k com.samples.HelloAndroidGeek" specifies the project's package name. The "-t 2" specifies the Target ID of the new project, "2" being the Target ID for an Android version 1.5 program. You can see more about these Target IDs by entering the command, "android list targets." Finally, the "-p /home/username/AndroidProjects/HelloAndroid/Geek" specifies the directory to create all of the project's subdirectories and files in. This creates the necessary directory structure and build file for your project to easily build your Android application (see Figure 11.5).

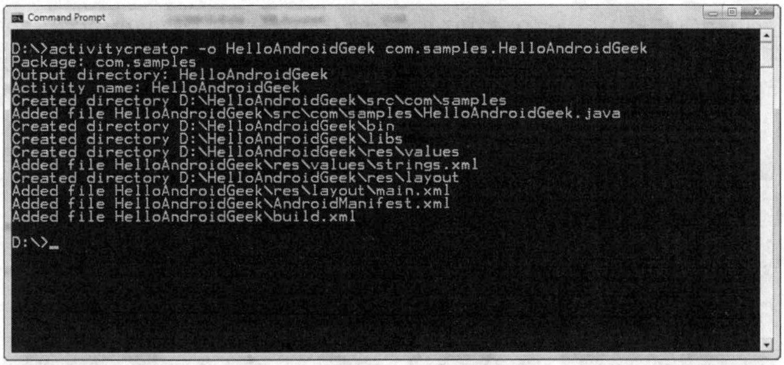

FIGURE 11.5
Running android script output.

If you navigate to the src/com/samples folder inside the HelloAndroidGeek folder, you will find that a Java source code file named HelloAndroidGeek.java has been generated for you. Edit the source file using your favorite editor so that it looks similar to the following code (don't worry about understanding what the code does—that's the focus of the next chapter):

```
package com.samples;
import android.app.Activity;
import android.os.Bundle;
import android.widget.TextView;

public class HelloAndroidGeek extends Activity
{
    /** Called when the activity is first created. */
```

```
@Override
public void onCreate(Bundle savedInstanceState)
{
    super.onCreate(savedInstanceState);
    TextView textView = new TextView(this);
    textView.setText("Hello, Android Geek");
    setContentView(textView);
}
}
```

The easiest way to build your application is to open a command prompt and run the command "ant -v debug" from the HelloAndroidGeek project folder (see Figure 11.6). You notice that in the project folder is a file named build.xml. This file contains tasks to compile the code and package it using tools from JDK and Android SDK. The command invokes a build by using the build.xml file and generates the necessary binaries in the bin folder.

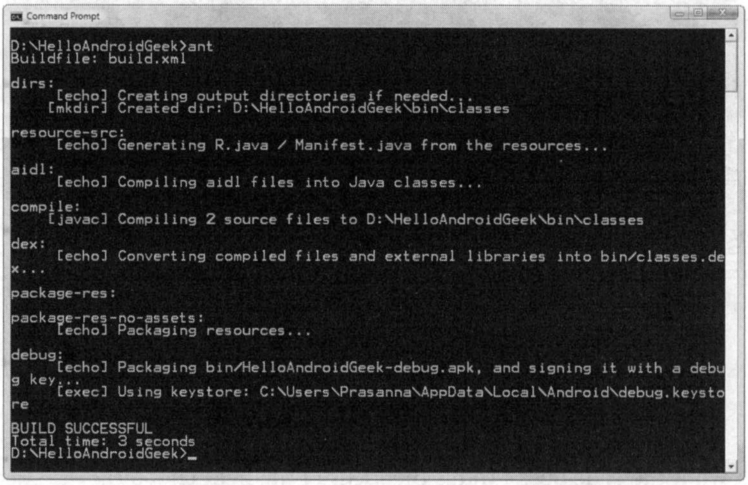

FIGURE 11.6
Running ant *to build the project.*

With the build complete, the bin folder now contains (among other files) a file named classes.dex file and a file named HelloAndroidGeek-debug.apk. The classes.dex file is a Dalvik executable file and is packaged with other required resources into the HelloAndroidGeek-debug.apk Android package file.

The next step is to deploy the Android package file to the device emulator. The Android device emulator is an emulation of an Android handset. This helps you test your application before you deploy it to a physical handset. Before you can run the emulator, you need to create an Android Virtual Device. The following command does this:

```
android create avd -t 2 -n G1Emu -p
➥/home/<username>/AndroidProjects/G1Emu
```

The "-t 2" tells the android script that the target device is running the "Cupcake" version of android (v1.5). The "-n G1Emu" gives the AVD a name, and the "-p" parameter tells the script which directory to put the new AVD in.

The Android emulator is a powerful tool with many options. You can see a list of those options with the command "emulator -help | less" on Linux or just "emulator -help" on Windows.

To deploy the application, start the emulator by running the command "emulator -avd G1Emu" on the command line. This starts the Android device emulator (see Figure 11.7).

FIGURE 11.7

Running the Android emulator.

Now you can deploy the application to the emulator by running the command "adb -e install HelloAndroidGeek-debug.apk" in a new command prompt window (see Figure 11.8). (If you want to deploy directly to your connected Android device, use "-d" instead of "-e" in the command.)

FIGURE 11.8

Deploying the application to the emulator.

This installs the newly created application in the Android device emulator. Now you can run the application by invoking it from the list of programs in the emulator. This displays the greeting message "Hello, Android Geek" from your first Android application, as shown in Figure 11.9.

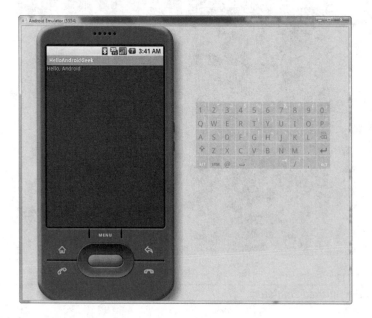

FIGURE 11.9

Android application running in the emulator.

Creating an Application Using Eclipse

Now that you've created your first Android application the hard way, let's look at how to create the same application using Eclipse. Eclipse shields a lot of the steps that you did previously in creating your Android application. Most of the command-line tools that you used to build your application are available as part of the IDE when you develop an Android application using Eclipse.

To create a new Android application in Eclipse, you must start by creating a project in Eclipse.

1. Open the **File** menu and click **New**, **Project**. This displays the New Project Wizard dialog, shown in Figure 11.10.

FIGURE 11.10

New Project Wizard dialog in Eclipse.

2. Select **Android**, **Android Project** as the project type and click **Next**.

3. Enter the project name as **HelloAndroidGeek**.

4. Choose a "Build Target" of "Android 1.5."

5. In the properties, enter the application name as "HelloAndroidGeek." the package name as **com.samples**, and the activity name as **HelloAndroidGeek**.

6. Click **Finish**. Eclipse generates the project files and the necessary directory structure, as shown in Figure 11.11.

FIGURE 11.11

Eclipse project directory structure.

Open the default generated HelloAndroidGeek.java file from the project explorer and replace the contents with the sample we used for the previous example.

To run the application in the emulator, click the **Run** icon in the toolbar or invoke Run by pressing **Ctrl+F11**. The first time you run the application in the emulator, you get the Run As dialog box, shown in Figure 11.12.

This dialog box appears because a project file needs to have a Run Configuration that configures how the application is executed. In the **Run As** dialog box, choose **Android Application** and click **OK**. This creates a run configuration with defaults for the project and executes the project by launching the emulator.

You can customize how the Android application runs when executed from Eclipse by editing the Run Configuration settings. Click **Run** and then **Run Configurations**. This displays the Run Configurations window (see Figure 11.13). Click the **HelloAndroidGeek Run Configuration** created under the

Android Application section. This displays various settings, including options that you can set for the launched emulator that runs your application.

FIGURE 11.12
Eclipse Run As dialog.

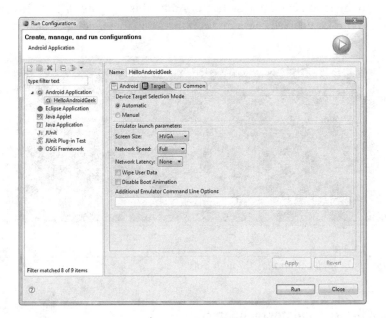

FIGURE 11.13
Android Run Configuration options.

Introduction to Android SDK Tools

In the previous sections, you read about a few tools in the commands used to create your simple application. Let us get some more information on how to use them and see what other commonly used tools are part of the Android SDK and the functionalities provided by them.

Android Debug Bridge (adb)

Android Debug Bridge is a tool that enables you to manipulate the Android emulator or device. In the previous section we used the Android Debug Bridge to install the sample application in the emulator. It has a useful set of commands that you can execute to do a variety of tasks, including copy files, run shell commands, and install or uninstall applications using Android Debug Bridge. The Android Debug Bridge commands require a device or emulator in a connected state. If there's no device or emulator and you attempt to run a command, you will get a message indicating that no device is present. After you have connected an emulator or device, you can start issuing the necessary commands to perform tasks on the emulator or device.

For example you can run the `adb shell` command to open a command shell to the Linux operating system of Android (see Figure 11.14). This enables you to run Linux shell commands on the Android emulator or device.

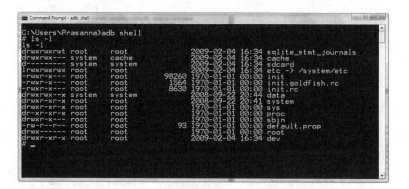

FIGURE 11.14
Running Linux shell commands through adb.

Android Device Emulator (emulator)

The Android Device Emulator enables you to emulate an Android handset. This gives you a way to deploy your Android application and test it before you release it to the market. In the previous section we ran our sample application using the emulator. It emulates all the features of the handset and provides a way to emulate various events. You can also invoke other applications and access various functionalities in the emulator.

You invoke the emulator by double-clicking it or by running the command `emulator` in the command prompt. You can also emulate events such as receiving an SMS or receiving a phone call.

To emulate these external events, `telnet` to the emulator and raise the necessary events. (Telnet is a command line utility that can be used to connect to remote system. In this instance we can use telnet to connect to the running emulator.) For example, to emulate an incoming call or receipt of an SMS, follow these steps:

1. Start the Android device emulator with the command `emulator`.

2. Open a command prompt and find out which port the emulator is running on by executing the command `adb devices` (see Figure 11.15).

FIGURE 11.15

Output of the `adb devices` command.

3. Next, run the `telnet localhost <port number>` command and connect to the port. For example, in Figure 11.15, the emulator is using port 5554. So to use Telnet, you run the command `telnet localhost 5554`.

4. When you're connected, you can initiate an incoming call on the emulator by running the Telnet command `gsm call <phone number>` (see Figure 11.16).

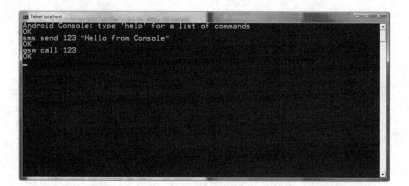

FIGURE 11.16

Running a Telnet command to initiate an incoming call.

This simulates an incoming phone call from the phone number specified in the command, as shown in Figure 11.17.

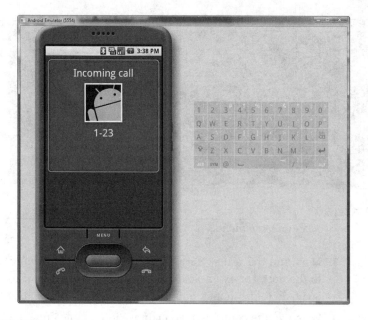

FIGURE 11.17

Incoming call on the emulator.

5. If you want to initiate an SMS to the emulator, run the Telnet command sms <phone number> <message>.

Make SD Card (mksdcard)

When you create databases or log files, you often want to save them to an SD card. The Make SD Card tool enables you to create a disk image to simulate an SD card for the emulator. To create an SD card, run the command mksdcard 1024M img. This creates an SD card disk image named img with 1024MB capacity. When you run the emulator, pass the -sdcard argument and pass the image you want to use as the SD card for the emulator (see Figure 11.18).

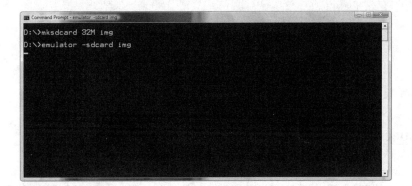

FIGURE 11.18
Creating and loading an SD card image.

Dalvik Debug Monitor Service (ddms)

Dalvik Debug Monitor Service is a tool that assists you in debugging your application. It uses Android Debug Bridge to connect to a device and help you debug applications running inside a Dalvik virtual machine. Using the Dalvik Debug Monitor Service, you can monitor thread and heap information, move files to and from the device or emulator, simulate incoming calls and SMS, send location information to simulate GPS information, and more. You can access some of these functionalities using the Android Debug Bridge, but Dalvik Debug Monitor Service provides a user interface and makes it easier to perform these tasks.

Start the Dalvik Debug Monitor Service by running the command ddms at the command prompt. Make sure you run the command from the tools folder of the Android SDK because it requires access to some libraries in the Android SDK folder. This launches the Dalvik Debug Monitor Service and displays the interface shown in Figure 11.19.

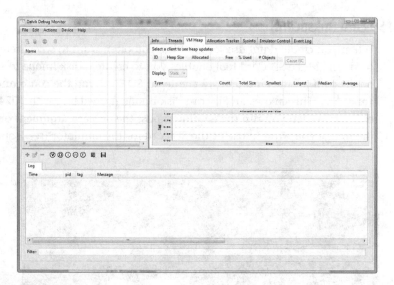

FIGURE 11.19

Dalvik Debug Monitor Service.

When you start the emulator, the Dalvik Debug Monitor Service displays information about the applications invoked and shows a details log file of log messages. You can select an application to view the threads executing and memory allocated for that application. For example, Figure 11.20 shows the threads executing for our sample application.

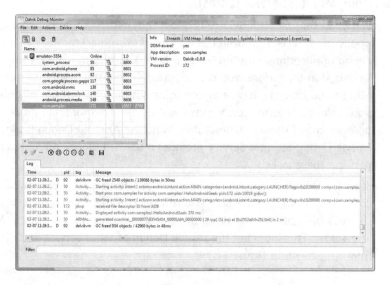

FIGURE 11.20

Debug information for an application.

As can be seen in Figure 11.20, when your simple "Hello Android Geek" application is running, there are several concurrent threads executing. In the bottom frame you can see a list of them, denoted by their process IDs ("pid") and their name ("tag"). The topmost of them seen is the "dalvikvm" thread running garbage collection ("GC") so as to recover some memory from objects that are no longer needed.

Your program is the "Activity" thread and you can see a sequence of "activities" (surprise!) running where the program instantiates the objects that make up your application. Also seen are various "housekeeping" threads running such as the "jdwp" and "ARMAs..." threads doing their thing to keep the Android emulator running as you expect it to.

Suffice it to say that a sophisticated system such as Android runs many different threads of programming code that make the cell phone behave as we expect it to. There are always multiple background tasks running to do things like monitor your GPS position, keep memory clean and available, write pixels to the screen, etc.

Android Asset Packaging Tool (aapt)

The Android Asset Packaging Tool is used to create, update, and view archive files in JAR, ZIP, or APK format. You can use it to examine the files in an Android package file. For example, running the command aapt 1 <<Android package file>> lists the files contained in our package file, as shown in Figure 11.21.

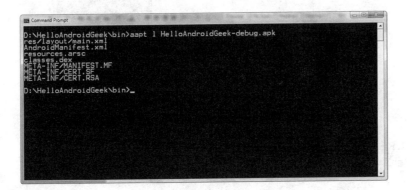

FIGURE 11.21
Android Asset Packaging tool listing package contents.

Hierarchy Viewer (hierarchyviewer)

The Hierarchy Viewer tool helps you optimize the user interface. It displays a tree view of the elements in the user interface and a wireframe view of the user interface. It also enables you to select elements in the tree view and inspect the properties of the user interface elements.

For example, to display the Hierarchy Viewer tool for the sample application, run the emulator and run the sample application we created. Next, run the command `hierarchyviewer` on a command line. This displays a user interface with a list of devices and a list of windows. Select the device listed for the emulator and to see a list of active windows. Select the window named `com.samples/com.samples/HelloAndroidGeek`, which is the interface for the sample application we created. Click the button *Load View Hierarchy*. This displays a layout view window, as shown in Figure 11.22.

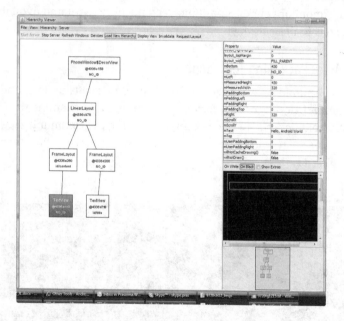

FIGURE 11.22
Hierarchy Viewer.

The Hierarchy Viewer tool also has a pixel-perfect view that you can toggle. You can use this to display the device window and a magnified view of the device window. The Hierarchy Viewer also enables you to see an image on top of the view, to design a user interface based on an image mockup.

UI/Application Exerciser Monkey

If the name of this tool brings a picture of a monkey clicking and playing with your application without any knowledge on what is happening, you've got it right. This tool tests your application by generating random events such as clicks and touches, to stress-test your application.

For example, running the command adb shell monkey -p com.android.camera 500 generates 500 random events to the camera application in the emulator (see Figure 11.23). You can see the camera application invoked in the emulator and random options in the camera application are selected and clicked. Similarly, you can generate random events to stress-test your application.

FIGURE 11.23
Running UI/Application Exerciser Monkey.

Trace View

Often you want to find out bottlenecks in your application to improve the performance of your application. Profiling your code in this way allows you to find out the parts of your application that need to be improved. While creating your application, you can write code to output trace information by profiling your application. The information contains details about the methods called and the time it took for the execution. This information is written to a binary format file. With the Trace View tool, you can load this file and examine the contents (see Figure 11.24).

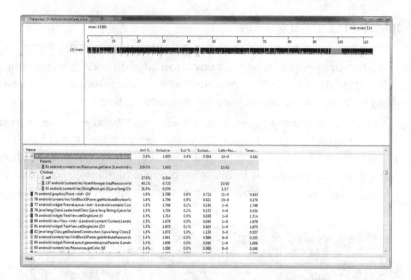

FIGURE 11.24

Trace View.

If you suspect that your code is running slower than it should be, the profiling tool is useful for locating where the slow code (aka the bottlenecks) exists. Our example has no bottlenecks, but it is still interesting to see where most of the CPU time is spent. According to this figure, you can see that the most time was spent in the "77 – android/widget/FrameLayout.<init>..." thread, where 1.746 of the total 13.801 milliseconds were spent.

SQLite

The SQLite tool helps you manage databases used in your Android application. SQLite is a database engine that has a low memory footprint and can run on low resources. This makes SQLite a preferred tool to create and work with databases that can be used in your Android applications. The SQLite tool that comes with the Android SDK allows you to run different commands to manage your database. You can run commands to examine the database and dump the contents of the database, etc.

Closing the Door

This chapter explained how to set up a development environment for your Android applications. It also explained how to create a very basic application using either ANT or Eclipse.

Developing Mobile Web Applications

I f you do a Google search on "What is a web application?" you will find more than 7,000 web pages that attempt to answer the question. The most common answer is that (1) it is an application that is accessed via a web browser over a network. The beauty of this definition is that, if designed carefully and targeted to the least common denominator of all web browsers, the application can run anywhere a browser is run, requiring no software modifications on the client side. Using this definition, a simple forms-based calculator is a web application.

Others insist that a real web application (2) also involves custom modifications to the browser, removing the advantage of ubiquity that definition 1 provides, but offering the capability to fine-tune the behavior of the client side of the application (caching data, providing direct access to local databases, and so on).

Still others say that a web application is (3) any program written to run on a client machine (such as your Android-powered cellphone) that also accesses its data from a remote machine (as Google Maps does). For the purposes of this book, we choose to accept all three definitions, but we focus on a combination of definitions 2 and 3: designing an Android program that uses the built-in WebKit browser to work with the server hosting the web application.

Designing, developing, and deploying mobile web applications is a complicated topic, and one chapter of this book is not sufficient to fully explore it. Multiple books have been and are being written to thoroughly describe many of the major topics involved in creating such applications. Countless websites also document the tools, protocols, and developer APIs that factor into the creative process of designing web applications.

With these facts in mind, consider this chapter a high-level overview of the process of designing mobile web applications, with suggestions and pointers to sources that can complete your knowledge of creating these important applications. Along the way, we touch on relevant issues briefly but orderly so that you can first use the simple examples and suggestions, and then build on them as you gain more knowledge. At the end of the chapter, we list websites that address all the issues raised.

By the end of the chapter, you will also have accumulated enough information to design web content that looks good on the T-Mobile G1 and other Android-powered cellphones. You'll also get tips for enhancing the performance of your web application's content when it is actually being rendered on the cellphone.

In designing web applications targeted to Android-powered cellphones, a few general principles foster a good experience with the application. The web application model involves two sides—the client side and the server side—so it's important to clearly indicate which side is being described. First, we address the client side, which is the Android cellphone.

Client Code

One principle that comes into play as you plan your application involves using the built-in tools and user interface (UI) methods of Android, to make the experience familiar to your target audience. Using the tools Android provides for you works better than reinventing the wheel. The Android framework provides a powerful, capable web browser that supports HTML/CSS and JavaScript, and that you can embed in your application as a WebView. Using code already written for you makes for small, tight applications—and the smaller and tighter your code is, the easier it is to test, debug, and deploy.

geek speak

WebView: WebView, as its name implies, allows you to display web content within your application. You can use it to display web pages or create your own mini web browser within your application. It provides methods for most of the functionalities that browsers support such as navigation, text search, etc.

The built-in Android web browser is Mobile Safari. It uses the open source WebKit plug-in to render the HTML/CSS web pages for viewing. WebKit also provides a plug-in architecture for scripting languages such as JavaScript. To better understand what this means to you, the web developer (or webmaster, as some prefer to be called), it's good to get a glimpse of the lowest level of detail that your server receives from Android when an Android-powered phone user requests your server's home page.

In creating web content that looks good and functions properly, it helps to know what specific browser is accessing your website. Simply put, when you visit a web page using the Android browser, Android sends a browser request packet to the server containing strings of data. This data includes information that the server needs to service the request. At minimum, this includes the page being requested and information about the kind of browser making the request.

The User-Agent

The user-agent is the client application that sends a web request. This information is sent with the browser request and allows the server to send different content based on the client. For example, the user-agent helps you detect the type of web browser sending the request. To understand this further, let us send a test request for a web page.

The actual URL requested during this test was http://192.168.0.5/, which is a local web server on my home network. Within the browser request is the host's address (192.168.0.5); the page being requested is /, or the home page of that host machine.

Let us look at the textual representation of a browser request to understand what information is sent with the browser request. The first line displays the type of web request and the protocol used (in this instance HTTP) followed by some attributes and their values

```
GET / HTTP/1.1
Host:            192.168.0.5
Accept-Encoding: gzip
Accept:          text/xml,application/xml,application/xhtml+xml,
                 text/html;q=0.9,text/plain;q=0.8,image/png,*/*;q=0.5
User-Agent:      Mozilla/5.0 (Linux; U; Android 1.1; en-us; dream)
                 AppleWebKit/525.10+ (KHTML, like Gecko) Version/3.0.4
                 Mobile Safari/523.12.2
Accept-Language: en-US
Accept-Charset:  utf-8, iso-8859-1, utf-16, *;q=0.7
```

Of particular importance is the User-Agent: attribute that the default Android
browser sends to every server it requests a page from. It's like a signature
telling the server what type of browser is requesting the page; thus, it allows
the server to refine how it prepares the page before sending back the requested
page.

Yellow Box

The sample PHP server script presented later in this chapter demonstrates how the
server uses the User-Agent: attribute to modify an HTML text area so that it fits
nicely into the small G1's screen area.

We can observe some interesting points about the user agent string Android
sends to every server that it requests web pages from. The entire string is a tes-
tament to the open architecture of Android: Eight different companies and
products are expressed in this unusually long user agent string! What are
these, and why does the Android browser use them to describe itself?

- **Mozilla**—The Mozilla Foundation is an organization that provides support for various open source projects. This organization makes the
  commonly used browsers Mozilla and Firefox, as well as the
  HTML/CSS-rendering engine Gecko.

- **Linux**—This is the operating system upon which all of Android is built.
  Much of Android's power as a cellphone and computing platform is
  attributable to this small, powerful operating system.

- **Android**—This name represents the entire software stack of the G1 and
  other cellphones like it.

- **Dream**—HTC (manufacturer of the T-Mobile G1) uses this alternate
  name to designate the G1 cellphone.

- **AppleWebKit**—This is an HTML/CSS-rendering engine similar to Gecko and KHTML. It's also known simply as WebKit. Apple Computing was a significant contributer to the development of the kit, so the company name is prepended to the name.

- **KHTML**—This is the original open source rendering engine from which the WebKit was derived.

- **Gecko**—This is the name of the Mozilla HTML/CSS-rendering engine. (See the first item in this list.)

- **Mobile Safari**—This is Apple Computing's open-source browser designed for hand-held computers and cellphones.

So why is all this information sent to servers on the World Wide Web every time Android requests a page, a graphic, or some other WWW object type? The reason is simple: to give the server enough information to properly create or prepare the page so that it looks good on the cellphone. Webmasters analyzing their server logs can also use this information to gather statistics on the kinds of devices and browsers that are accessing their websites. You can be sure of one thing: If most users visiting websites are using tiny-screen cellphone devices, webmasters will feel market pressure to design their websites to better accommodate the handsets.

Each of these names (and the other embedded information in the user-agent string) actually represents a set of openly documented functions and features that webmasters can find on the Internet. (See the upcoming section "External Links.") Webmasters can then use these functions and features to design web content that looks good and functions well on the Android handset.

Of course, webmasters can simply ignore the user-agent string; this is likely the most common practice in designing web content. Designing web content for the specific quirks of every different web browser is a time-intensive task, and good reasons should support the choice to do this. In the case of web content for cellphones, an exception should be made for at least two reasons.

Whatever other reasons exist, the most important lies in the numbers: The increased usage of mobile devices indicate that, in the coming years, likely more people will use cellphone handsets to browse the Web than a large-screen PC. Also important is the fact that the media are so different: PC monitors can vary in size from 15 inches to 40 inches and beyond, with billions of pixels in thousands of colors to display web content. Cellphones, on the other hand, have significantly limited screen sizes, so a website that is specifically

12

designed to pack as much information as possible into a page intended to be rendered on one of the large screens will be difficult to navigate on a cell-phone screen.

When designing the client-side application code, keep in mind the nature of the client's connection with the server side. Because of its mobile nature, the link between the two can have spotty coverage. Therefore, the programmer of the client code must compensate for potential delays and outages in the con-nection, as well as find ways to preserve the data that is already being oper-ated on: either data that the server transmitted to the cellphone or data that was generated on the cellphone itself (such as form data).

Here, the Android framework provides powerful and automatic ways of pre-serving session data so that if your web application is interrupted (by a phone call, for example), the form the user is filling out doesn't have to be restarted and the data that has already been entered doesn't have to be re-entered. The designers of the Android API took careful note of these process-interrupting events and prepared for most of them, saving you from having to come up with solutions to these problems yourself.

So far, we have offered some general tips on how to write client code. Now it's time to cover some specifics and install the Android software development kit (SDK) on your workstation. Again, this is too complicated of a process to describe in this chapter: We recommend that you bookmark this page, use the link "Installing the Android SDK" at the end of this chapter to see how to download and install it, and then return to this page to create a simple web application using the Eclipse IDE and the Android SDK.

The web application that we create in this chapter is a simple one that enables you to do the following:

- You can embed the WebKit browser into a custom Android application that visits a specific server-based web application.

- When the web application runs, it presents a form enabling you to choose from a list of files to edit. Then it presents a form for actually editing a file remotely on the server.

Although this is simple in theory, computers are anything but simple in com-pleting the task. To create the sample code for the client side of this web appli-cation, follow these steps:

1. Using the Eclipse IDE, create an empty Android Project with **File, New, Project**.

2. Choose the **Android/Android Project Wizard** option. The New Project Wizard opens (see Figure 12.1).

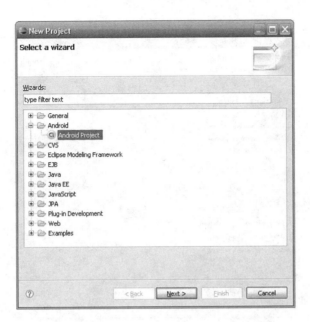

FIGURE 12.1

A new Android project starts with the Project Wizard, which walks you through setting up the new project.

3. Select **Android Project** and then click **Next**.

4. In the next window, set the following parameters, as shown in Figure 12.2.

   Project name: **WebApp**

   Contents: **Create New Project in Workspace**

   Make sure **Use Default Location** is checked

   Package name: **webApp.WebApp**

   Activity name: **WebApp**

   Application name: **WebApp**

5. After you've entered these parameters, click **Finish** to start the new project.

When the Wizard creates an Android project, it creates a subdirectory under your Eclipse workspace with the same name as the project. It also creates subdirectories under the project – res, src, etc.

FIGURE 12.2

Use the Project Wizard to set the parameters for your new Android project.

Within these subdirectories, the Wizard creates files that will properly build an application, but since the files are templates they have no functionality. In order for you to give your application the functionality that it requires, you need to replace these templated files with your own code. After the Wizard creates a new Android project called WebApp, you need to replace the contents of the following three files, under the WebApp directory with the provided code:

- AndroidManifest.xml
- res\layout\main.xml
- src\webApp.WebApp\WebApp.java

Tools such as the Android Market use the AndroidManifest.xml file to define what kinds of things your program will seek to do. This example needs to access the Internet, so that is why it is being modified.

The contents of AndroidManifest.xml should be as follows:

```
<?xml version="1.0" encoding="utf-8"?>
    <manifest xmlns:android="http://schemas.android.com/apk/res/android"
        package="webApp.WebApp"
        android:versionCode="1"
```

```
   android:versionName="1.0.0">
  <application android:icon="@drawable/icon"
    android:label="@string/app_name">
    <activity android:name=".WebApp"
      android:label="@string/app_name">
      <intent-filter>
        <action android:name="android.intent.action.MAIN" />
        <category android:name="android.intent.category.LAUNCHER" />
      </intent-filter>
    </activity>
  </application>
  <uses-permission android:name="android.permission.INTERNET" />
</manifest>
```

Our `AndroidManifest.xml` file differs from the Android Project Wizard's file by one line: the `uses-permission` line, which specifies that the application needs to be permitted to access the Internet. No surprise there!

To maintain tight control over what applications running on your handset can do, the engineers who designed Android use this file to control what functions and features of the cellphone the program is allowed to use.

Next up, the contents of the `res\layout\main.xml` file should be modified to define how we want the application's layout to look, as follows:

```
<?xml version="1.0" encoding="utf-8"?>
<LinearLayout xmlns:android="http://schemas.android.com/apk/res/android"
  android:layout_width="wrap_content"
  android:layout_height="wrap_content"
  android:orientation="vertical">
  <WebView
    android:id="@+id/webview"
    android:layout_width="fill_parent"
    android:layout_height="fill_parent"
  />
</LinearLayout>
```

Here, a WebView layout is defined so that it occupies the entire area of the application's main window. This is accomplished by setting the layout width and height to `fill_parent`. The simple application being designed here is nothing more than a wrapper for the WebKit browser, but you can easily expand it to include its own custom menus, and perhaps other views that differ from the embedded browser.

12

To keep things simple, here we simply embed the browser and present a shell of an application that you can expand later as your Java skills grow and develop.

Finally, the contents of the src\webApp.WebApp\WebApp.java file should be replaced with code that will properly function as a browser-like application. To do this, the template should be replaced with this code, as follows:

```java
package webApp.WebApp;

import android.app.Activity;
import android.os.Bundle;
import android.view.KeyEvent;
import android.webkit.WebView;
import android.webkit.WebViewClient;

public class WebApp extends Activity
{
  WebView webview;

  private class WebAppClient extends WebViewClient
  {
    @Override
    public boolean shouldOverrideUrlLoading(WebView view, String url)
    {
      view.loadUrl(url);
      return true;
    }
  }


  public boolean onKeyDown(int keyCode, KeyEvent event)
  {
    if ((keyCode == KeyEvent.KEYCODE_BACK) && webview.canGoBack())
    {
      webview.goBack();
      return true;
    }

    return super.onKeyDown(keyCode, event);
  }
```

12

```
    @Override
    public void onCreate(Bundle savedInstanceState)
    {
      super.onCreate(savedInstanceState);
      setContentView(R.layout.main);

      webview = (WebView) findViewById(R.id.webview);
      webview.setWebViewClient(new WebAppClient());
      webview.getSettings().setJavaScriptEnabled(true);
      webview.loadUrl("http://www.google.com/");          // Comment out
➥this line,
        // webview.loadUrl("http://192.168.0.1/red.php");  // uncomment and
➥modify the URL in this one
      }                                                    // to use the
➥server side code
    }                                                      // example later
➥in the text.
```

This code is designed to execute the WebKit browser within our application, enabling the user to navigate a website by clicking hyperlinks and pressing the Back button. Although it does nothing more than the standard web browser application that comes with Android, it enables us to modify it any way the web application design requires in the future. We simply need to add the code that overrides the standard browser behavior with our own custom-designed methods.

After replacing the three indicated files in the WebApp project, we can build the code, test it on the emulator, and then package it up to port to the Android cellphone. In keeping with the high-level nature of this chapter, we leave the details to you—you can explore the Google documentation on building an Android application in the links provided at the end of this chapter.

Server Code

Many different types of web servers service browser requests, so the principles presented in this chapter are generic instead of tailored to specific web servers. Each type has its own way of doing things, and it is beyond the scope of this book to give specific instructions for each web server type.

Suffice it to say that the modern web server provides different programmatic methods for reading the user-agent string (and all the other strings shown in the browser request), and code that parses, examines, and reacts to the content of those strings depends on the specific server the webmaster is using. The specific web server's documentation includes detailed information.

Having said that, this chapter focuses on *what* to do instead of *how* to do it, based on the user-agent string. For example, if the server determines that an Android-powered handset is requesting a web page, it should return a smaller, less dense HTML page. When designing web content to be rendered on small machines, *keep it simple.*

The code that runs on the web server is responsible for not only its half of the interactive nature of the web application, but also for issues such as authenticating the cellphone that is contacting it and providing a way for the cellphone user to download the client-side code. Although such client-side code can be distributed with public systems such as the Android Market, a business might not want to do this in some cases, instead preferring to maintain a more confidential relationship with those using the application.

The question then becomes, how is the client-side code loaded onto the cellphone in the first place? As long as the application is a properly signed application, it can appear as a simple hyperlink on a server download page. To install the application, the user simply must go into the application settings and allow the installation of nonmarket applications from unknown sources when installing one of these custom applications.

This is the sample server code, written in the common PHP web programming language:

```php
<?php
  $thedir="/home/bzimmerly/kill";
  $ext[1]="txt";
  $ext[0]="TXT";


  function head()
  {
    echo "<html>\n";
    echo "<head>\n";
    echo "<title>\n";
    echo "Remote Editor\n";
    echo "</title>\n";
    echo "</head>\n";
    echo "<body>\n";
  }
```

```php
function tail()
{
  echo "</body>\n";
  echo "</html>\n";
}

function reply($text)
{
  head();
  echo $text;
  echo "<br/>\n";
  echo "<a href=\"\">Back to editor</a>.\n";
  tail();
}

function txtarea($text)
{
  if(strpos($_SERVER['HTTP_USER_AGENT'],
      'Android') !== FALSE)
  {
    $Android=1;
    $rows=5;
    $cols=30;
  }
  else
  {
    $Android=0;
    $rows=30;
    $cols=80;
  }

  echo "<br/>\n";

  if($Android == 1)
  {
    echo "<span style=\"-webkit-box-shadow:10px 10px 5px #888;\">\n";
  }

  echo "<textarea name=\"mods\" rows=\"";
  echo $rows . "\" cols=\"" . $cols . "\">\n";
```

```php
    echo $text;
    echo "</textarea>\n";

    if($Android == 1)
    {
      echo "</span>\n";
    }

    echo "<br/>\n";
    echo "</form>\n";
}

function d2a($dir, $recurse)
{
  $me=basename($_SERVER['PHP_SELF']);
  $files=array();

  if($handle=opendir($dir))
  {
    while(false !== ($file=readdir($handle)))
    {
      if($file != "." &&
         $file != ".." &&
         $file != $me &&
         substr($file,0,1) != '.')
      {
        if(is_dir($dir. "/" . $file))
        {
          if($recurse)
          {
            $files=array_merge($files, d2a($dir. "/" .
                               $file,
                               $recurse));
          }
        }
        else
        {
          $file=$dir . "/" . $file;
          $files[]=preg_replace("/\/\//si", "/", $file);
        }
```

```
      }
    }

    closedir($handle);
    asort($files);
  }

  return $files;
}

syslog(LOG_INFO, "{$_SERVER['REMOTE_ADDR']}: Remote Edit Accessed.");

if($_SERVER['REQUEST_METHOD'] != 'POST')
{
  if(is_readable($thedir))
  {
    head();

    echo "<form action=\"" . $PHP_SELF;
    echo "\" method=\"post\">\n";
    echo "<select name=\"the_file\">\n";

    chdir($thedir);

    $filelist=d2a($thedir, true);

    foreach($filelist as $file)
    {
      $ex=substr(strrchr($file, '.'), 1);

      if(in_array($ex,$ext) && is_writable($file))
      {
        echo "<option value=\"$file\">$file</option>\n";
      }
    }

    echo "</select>\n";
    echo "<br/>\n";
    echo "<input type=\"submit\" name=\"open\"";
    echo "value=\"Open\"/>\n";
```

```
        txtarea("");
        tail();
      }
      else
      {
        reply("Error: Bad directory.\n");
      }
    }
    else if(isset($_POST['open']))
    {
      if(is_writable($_POST["the_file"]))
      {
        $file2open=fopen($_POST["the_file"], "r");
        $current_data=@fread($file2open,
                            filesize($_POST["the_file"]));
        $current_data=eregi_replace("</textarea>",
                                "<DO-NOT-EDIT>",
                                $current_data);

        head();

        echo "<form action=\"" . $PHP_SELF;
        echo "\" method=\"post\">\n";
        echo "<input type=\"hidden\" name=\"cur_file\" ";
        echo "value=\"" . $_POST["the_file"] . "\"/>\n";
        echo $_POST["the_file"];
        echo "<br/>\n";
        echo "<input type=\"submit\" name=\"save\" ";
        echo "value=\"Save\"/>\n";

        txtarea($current_data);
        tail();
        fclose($file2open);
      }
      else
      {
        reply("Error: Cannot open file.\n");
      }
    }
```

```
    else if(isset($_POST['save']))
    {
      if(is_writable($_POST["cur_file"]))
      {
        $file2ed=fopen($_POST["cur_file"], "w+");
        $data_to_save=$_POST["mods"];
        $data_to_save=eregi_replace("<DO-NOT-EDIT>",
                                    "</textarea>",
                                    $data_to_save);
        $data_to_save=stripslashes($data_to_save);

        if(fwrite($file2ed,$data_to_save))
        {
          reply("File saved.\n");
          fclose($file2ed);
        }
        else
        {
          reply("Error: Cannot save file.\n");
          fclose($file2ed);
        }
      }
      else
      {
        reply("Error: Cannot save file.\n");
      }
    }
?>
```

When accessed from the Android cellphone, this web program senses that the Android text is in the User-Agent: attribute. It automatically adjusts the size of the input text-area form to fit the smaller screen of the device, and it adds the box-shadow effect to the text area to enhance its appearance.

Security and Authentication

Fortunately, security between clients and servers on the World Wide Web is mainly handled through public key encryption. This encryption method is a built-in feature of most web servers and clients, including Android. As a programmer, you need not concern yourself with public key encryption, other than making sure that your browser requests use the SSL protocol by prefacing every URL with the `https` (s for security) tag. Remember, if you use `http`, it will *not* be a secure connection.

Servers handle user authentication in diverse ways, most involving a user ID and password known to the server's user database. Handling this authentication is simple, and most server documentation includes code examples.

Error Handling

Web applications are more complicated than the simple, one-dimensional client requests and server replies in the file model that predominated during the early years of the Internet and the World Wide Web. In those days, the Internet was much like (and was even called) an Information Superhighway. Most websites were like simple billboards that decorated that superhighway.

Times have changed. Processes have become richer and more powerful. In a typical web-centric application, the following sequence of events occurs between the client and server.

1. The client calls the server, requesting a secure connection.
2. The server replies to the client with a session token, allowing a secure, encrypted session to occur between the two.
3. The client passes login information back to the server.
4. The server authenticates the client and replies with a My Page for the client to use.
5. The client fills out a form and submits it to the server.
6. The server checks the form for potential errors. If the form is clean, the server does something with the form, such as calling an external process to order products that the client wants to purchase.
7. The server returns another page to the client, with information on the status of the ordering process.

During this back-and-forth process, problems can arise in several ways:

- A phone call interruption
- Loss of a signal from the cell tower
- Interruption of the session because of a network problem
- Invalid data on the form the client submits
- Outdated server SSL certificates

The Android framework and the server's error-recovery mechanisms handle some of these problems automatically, but your code must properly handle many of them. This is one reason why the Android team chose Java as the primary development language for web applications. Java provides a rich and powerful set of features that catch error conditions and provide an easy way of properly handling them.

Server code can also be written in the Java programming language. Indeed, much of the World Wide Web currently uses Java for dynamic server content. Many examples show Java code used for writing applications that run on servers on websites such as IBM's developerWorks. (See the link in the upcoming section "External Links.")

The new field of "cloud computing" attempts to clarify issues for vendors of web applications and client companies. By contracting out web services to cloud computing vendors, the times of peak usage of your web applications can be maximized. When the times where fewer people are making use of your web application, you aren't billed at the same rate and are therefore able to save money.

Many companies are offering these cloud computing services for reasonable, almost utility like-rates, similar to what an electric company or water company would charge. You can find more of this kind of information on the IBM developerWorks website.

Designing Web Content for Android

Designing web content in general requires knowledge about how most browsers render the various web protocols; HTML, CSS, etc. Likewise, designing web content for specific browsing targets like small Android-powered cell-phones requires knowing how they render the same protocols. This knowledge enables you to make wise choices so that your web content looks and functions great under Android. With this in mind, let us now review the web protocols and how much support for them is provided by Android.

WebKit Support for Advanced CSS

The Android browser implements subsets of the World Wide Web Consortium's CSS 2.1 and 3 specifications (www.w3.org/TR/css3-roadmap/). According to design, web browsers are designed to simply ignore any CSS property that they don't support, so when you test any of the specifications defined on your own web pages, the Android browser gracefully ignores some of them.

It is beyond the scope of this book to reproduce the highly detailed specifications found on the Consortium's website, but an exciting example should interest you enough to explore the technology in greater depth. This example involves the `box-shadow` property for making the browser automatically put a shadow around text and graphics.

You can read about it in depth at www.w3.org/TR/css3-background/#the-box-shadow. You can also see a demonstration of the feature by creating the following small HTML text file, installing it on your web server, and having your cellphone browse it:

```
A Demonstration of box-shadowing:

<html>
<head>
<title>Android: Webkit Extentions</title>
</head>
<body>

<span
  style="-webkit-box-shadow:10px 10px 5px #888;">
Box shadowed image...
</span>

<img src="image.gif"
  style="-webkit-box-shadow:10px 10px 5px #888;">

</body>
</html>
```

When this small snippet of HTML code is rendered on your Android cellphone, the text and the image file will have a shadow around it.

You'll notice that the style property `-webkit-box-shadow` differs from the CSS3 specification. If you want to read up on more specific details of the WebKit standard, see http://developer.apple.com/safari/library/documentation/AppleApplications/Reference/SafariCSSRef/Articles/StandardCSSProperties.html. Not all of those specifications are supported by Android, but most are.

WebKit Support for JavaScript

JavaScript is the primary programming language used on web pages and executed on the client side of the application. Brendan Eich, of Netscape, invented the language in the early days of the World Wide Web (around the early 1990s), and it appeared in the Netscape Navigator version 2.0 browser.

Since then, all browsers of significance, including the Android browser, have incorporated JavaScript. The development of a standard document for the language started in late 1996 and that standard has since evolved into what is known as the ECMA Standard.

The WebKit JavaScript engine, called JavaScriptCore, is a separate framework from WebCore and WebKit. JavaScript provides a dynamic tool for reacting to important programmatic events such as mouseovers, mouse clicks, initial page loading, and so forth. It is a strongly-typed, object-oriented language, very similar to the Java programming language it was named after. Make no mistake about it, however: JavaScript is not Java.

As a scripting language, JavaScript is transmitted in source form from the server to the client (Android). Then it is compiled and executed on the fly when the page is loaded. To keep web applications that load into the browser executing quickly, code should remain small and short, and looping processes should not be incorporated into a web page's JavaScript code.

Common uses for JavaScript include generating dynamic menus, properly validating and formatting form data, and providing useful widgets that can appear on a web page such as a dynamic clock or calendar.

Performance Tips for Mobile Content

When developing web applications, you can do several things to make the user's experience browsing your website a pleasant one. We offer several major categories of useful tips, including techniques for optimal loading time and ways to make navigating the site a pleasant experience.

12

Optimal Loading Time

The time it takes for a web page to load is often the main factor in whether a user continues to browse your website. If pages take too long to load, a user might never return. How long is "too long" depends on the individual, but most people won't tolerate a load time of more than a minute on an average-speed broadband connection. To minimize loading time for your pages, also minimize the number and size of graphic files. Many tools for designing and editing graphic files include ways to reduce the size of the graphics while still maintaining an appealing visual. (See the "External Links" section of the chapter for links to some of them.)

When considering load time, keep in mind that very large (even book-length) HTML pages can be smaller than even a tiny graphic file. For example, consider the Project Gutenberg book *A Discourse of a Method for the Well Guiding of Reason, and the Discovery of Truth in the Sciences,* by Rene Descartes (www.gutenberg.org/files/25830/25830-h/25830-h.htm). This entire book in HTML form is only 154KB in size—about the size of an average graphic file. The moral is, a lot of text is good, but graphics are far more costly in terms of bandwidth.

Also, putting links to audio and video content on the page is better than posting the content itself. This speeds up the content-loading process by letting the person who is browsing your site *choose* to listen to or see the content. Many blogs and websites inadvisably stuff their sites full of videos that automatically start playing when the page is loaded. Avoid this practice unless the nature of your site dictates otherwise.

Simple Layout

A clean layout is an aesthetically pleasing design for a website and shares a common design with all other pages on it. One technique for obtaining that effect is to separate the presentation code of a website from content-using tools such as Cascading Style Sheets (CSS) and templates.

A good formula for designing a simple and clean layout is to design one page carefully and then convert it into a template. The server then can substitute the content into the template and send back the assimilated page to the requesting browser.

Clean Navigation

Clean navigation and a simple layout are closely related and are often both expressed in the design of the common template. When users visit your website, they will see a method of navigation used on the initial page; when they go to subsequent pages, they will want to see those links appear in the same position on those pages. The less you force the people visiting your site to learn new navigation techniques, the more they will like your site—and use it, if it interests them.

Another important tip for easy website navigation is to have a site map, showing a well-ordered outline of all the available web pages. If the site has too many pages to actually list them in a site map, it's good to have multiple-page site maps, to expand to deeper levels. For example, a company website site map can have lower-level departmental site maps linked off the main site map.

Another important navigation tool is a simple search form. Never underestimate the value of such a widget in helping people who are visiting your website find what they are looking for, especially if you're selling a large inventory of products from the site. You can easily implement features such as this using Google's capability to narrow a search within a specific domain; this is why many websites incorporate a simple search form that lets Google provide the programming muscle for searching the site. It's free and easy to use, so you really have no excuse for not using it.

Handling Broken Links

Broken links present an unprofessional look on a website. Avoid them as much as humanly possible. You should also create a customized 404 page that uses your clean template (described earlier) to return to the browser a useful page with the same navigational links and layout that users are accustomed to seeing throughout your website.

Tools are available for scanning websites and locating and reporting broken links, to help webmasters clean up their sites. Some of these are listed at the end of the chapter in the "External Links" section.

Obviously, maintaining a functional website with fresh content is a difficult task without using the proper tools. Along with tools for locating and reporting broken links, we have included a list of tools for many other aspects of web design, programming, and maintenance in the "External Links" section at the end of this chapter.

Spell-Checking

Websites that have spelling and grammatical errors also appear unprofessional. Good web development involves passing all textual content through spell-checking tools, such as those found in the commonly used Office suites. With content separated from the presentation portions of a website, it is a much easier task to pass the textual content through these tools without having to worry about HTML tags such as <span> getting flagged as a spelling error.

Many content management systems (CMS) are available for download and/or purchase, to simplify the task of maintaining a complex website. Good content management systems are web based, which means that they use the web for content generation. For example, they might allow reporters to type their columns in a web form (perhaps on the spot using Android), spell-check them, and save them so that a human editor can later edit them. Finally, they can be released for public display when ready.

Many university-based websites, such as those of Washington University (in St. Louis, Missouri) and Indiana University, use CMS to manage the entire

12

website remotely via the Web. If you visit these websites, you can see the common, template-based design that the CMS enforces.

External Links

One chapter can't provide all the information necessary for such a complicated topic. As we noted in the introduction to this chapter, entire books have been written to address both halves of the design of client/server systems, such as a web application. For more on the various issues we brought up in this chapter, look to the following books and websites.

Client Issues

Android Developers Documentation (http://developer.android.com/) is a website with specific information about the Android platform and is a great resource for tips and techniques for using Android as a client for web applications.

Java Home Page (http://java.sun.com/) and Java Programmers Documentation (http://java.sun.com/docs/books/tutorial/). Since Android programming is mainly done in the Java programming language, these two links are provided for reference.

JavaScript Programmers Documentation (www.javascript.com/) Web content makes use of this dynamic programming language and this link is provided for client-side programming reference as well.

Apple Computer's Developer Connection (http://developer.apple.com/) and WebKit Documentation (http://webkit.org/) A lot of information on Android's built-in browser can be found on these two websites.

The World Wide Web Consortium (w3.org) (http://www.w3.org/www.w3.org/) defines all of the necessary protocols that are used in creating web content.

Common Server Issues

Apache (http://apache.org/) is the most common open-source server technology used in the world.

Microsoft IIS (www.iis.net/) is the preferred server technology of many in the business world.

Open Source CMS (www.opensourcecms.com/) is a website with a lot of information on open source content management systems.

Graphic Editing Tools—Adobe Photoshop (www.adobe.com/products/photoshop/family/) and Graphic Editing Tools—Open Source, "The Gimp" (www.gimp.org/) are two of the most commonly used tools for designing and editing graphics used in web content.

PHP (www.php.net/) is a powerful and commonly used server-side scripting language for designing dynamic web content.

The Internet Engineering Task Force (www.ietf.org/) is another great website for information on web development and sever side issues.

The W3C Link Checker for Finding Broken Links (http://validator.w3.org/checklink) is a useful tool for scanning your website and locating broken links.

Miscellaneous Tools (www.d.umn.edu/itss/support/Training/Online/webdesign/tools.html) and IBM developerWorks (www.ibm.com/developerworks/) are two websites that provide up-to-date and in-depth technical information on web development tools and techniques.

Washington University (www.wustl.edu/) and Indiana University (www.indiana.edu/) are two university websites (mentioned in the chapter) that use content management systems for managing their web content.

Advanced Android Apps

A dvanced applications are born when people come up with good ideas about what useful work can be accomplished by the hardware that is available. In order to stimulate those ideas, it is important to know what devices exist in your Android cellphone. For example, the fact that a magnetic compass is one of the devices built into the cellphone implies that a program can know what direction it is pointing at relative to the Earth. Advanced applications that display the correct view of the stars in the sky that the user is looking at are therefore possible. By combining current data from the magnetic compass and the real time clock, an accurate sky map can be prepared and displayed for the user. This chapter enumerates the devices found in the G1 Android cellphone as a means of stimulating good application ideas.

Ultimate Portability

One of the amazing things about computers is that, whereas all other machines are amplifiers of our senses and muscles, computers are amplifiers of our minds. Of course, as useful as they are, all computers are only as good as the software running on them. Some computers are totally dedicated to one specific task, such as the computer that monitors the health of your automobile engine and alerts you to problems with it. Others are general-purpose computers, capable of a wide variety of tasks.

Because modern cellphone networks are digitally based, all modern cellphones have a built-in computer. Most of these computers are special-purpose computers because they are dedicated to operating only the phone features. A few others are more general purpose in nature and contain some other programs, most with simple PDA and game-playing functionality. But a select few are truly general-purpose computers residing in the highly portable form factor of a cell phone. One of these is, of course, the subject of this book.

Modern Android-based cellphones are among the most useful of portable computers, due in no small part to some of the amazing programs written to take advantage of the machine's capabilities—that is, the devices built into the machine that it accesses programmatically.

The original Android cellphone, the HTC/T-Mobile G1, is an intricate collection of devices that enable clever programmers to design advanced applications. A quick review of these devices provides a glimpse of what the machine is really capable of:

- Multiple radios

    G3 Cellular, for cellular and Internet service

    Bluetooth, for short-range local service with BT-enabled devices

    Wi-Fi, for access to Internet services via a local Wi-Fi hotspot

    GPS, for getting locational fixes from GPS satellites

- Multiple sensory devices

    Microphone, for audio input

    Accelerometer, for sensing motion in space-time

    Magnetic compass, for sensing direction relative to Earth

13

- Multiple I/O devices

    Touch screen, which provides the device with a tactile sense

    Color display, the main output device for visually oriented humans

    Keyboard, the main device for text input

    Loudspeaker, the main device for audio output

    Earphones, the secondary device for audio output

- Multiple computer resources

    Dual-core processor—ARM 9 and ARM 11 32-bit CPUs

    Multimegabytes of RAM, for "working" storage while running

    Multigigabytes of SD FLASH, for secondary storage of data

    528MHz clock, a fast clock for a cellphone-size device

Couple all that with a flexible and powerful base operating system that enables software programs to use those devices in an efficient and coordinated manner, and you end up with a surprisingly sophisticated little device.

Although not strictly considered an application, we would not be faithful to our book's title designation if we didn't give well-deserved kudos to Linus Torvalds and his mighty crew of developers. Always remember, Android is Linux—*and* Linux is awesome!

Lastly, in our discussion of the "devices" that make up the Android cellphone, let's not forget the most amazing peripheral device of all: the Internet itself.

Make Contact

John Burdette Gage, the fifth employee of Sun Microsystems, is often credited with coining the phrase, "The Network is the Computer!" This profound observation is correct. The seemingly seamless operation of the cellphone computer when it operates on data that was retrieved from other computers on the Internet gives us an impression of an all-powerful information appliance that is a welcome addition to our complicated lives. With the world's information literally at our fingertips, we can make better-informed decisions about manifold issues that we face at the current moment.

Just as a good peripheral device adds significant value to the system, the Internet essentially adds a vast array of powerful computers and their

13

resources to your Android cellphone, as long as Android applications know how to talk to it. And thanks to the dedicated efforts of hundreds of computer programmers, Android does know how to talk to it.

Currently, specific software tools housed on the Internet have been integrated into the functionality of your Android cellphone so that you can edit data either with a workstation running an Internet browser or using the cellphone itself and then having the software automatically synchronize them. These Google-specific tools are all related to your Google-specific account. The applications kept in synchronization are Gmail, your contact lists, your calendar, and your financial portfolios. The synchronization that occurs here is automatic, so you don't need to do anything to make it happen.

With such a rich list of integrated devices, base software, and access to countless databases and servers with raw computing power through the digital network connection of the Internet, creative people are coming up with all sorts of ideas for how to use them—and many of those people are not even programmers.

If you are one of those nonprogrammers with a good idea for an advanced application, why not get on one of the Google Group Forums (see the links at the end of this chapter) and describe your idea? Perhaps a programmer will agree with you and be willing to turn your idea into reality.

This idea stage is when people connect the dots (device capabilities with human needs) and come up with useful application ideas that can exploit the power of these devices. Remember that every great technological advance that we enjoy today began as an idea in somebody's head. The only thing preventing a good idea from becoming reality is the desire and drive on the part of that somebody—go ahead, make contact with the Android community!

A Few Programmer/Analyst Tips

For programmers or systems analysts thinking about how to implement these ideas, it's good to think of the Android cellphone as just the displayer of what you want users to see. Even though the computer in the Android cellphone is a powerful one, there's no reason to burden the handset with excessive number crunching, database lookups, or even data collating from multiple sources on the Internet; those functions are best done by a powerful, dedicated server.

When that server has done its job and is ready to present output to the user, you can concentrate on writing the Android application to use it. One tip for converting a good idea to an Android application is to write it as a normal application for a PC and then have that converted to use the Android cellphone as the remote input/output device. Creating and testing a good idea in this way is significantly easier than starting at the finish line of the Android cellphone itself.

Another useful tip is to study the Google applications that are designed to automatically synchronize data between a Google account and the cellphone. This is a good model to emulate in any advanced application you are working on. (More information on this is comes later in the chapter, in the section "Creating Advanced Apps.")

How to Get Advanced Apps

When Google, HTC, T-Mobile, and the Open Handset Alliance released Android to the world in the form of the G1 cellphone, they launched the Android Market as well. The Android Market is an online web application that enables program developers to directly give away (and sell) their creations to users of the handsets. You can visit the Cyrket Android Market Browser, http://www.cyrket.com, with your workstation browser if you want to see the status of the Android Market on the larger screen of your PC.

Thousands of applications are already only a few clicks (or screen taps) away from running on your device. Some of these are very advanced applications. Much of this chapter focuses on these applications and describes why we, the authors of this book, consider them so advanced.

So what qualifies an application as "advanced"? The short answer is that this is an arbitrary and subjective designation, totally the opinion of those who use it. We all have our preferences and diverse tastes. One person might want the most advanced calculator program that can be downloaded, whereas another might be interested only in programs that help him keep close tabs on his stock portfolio. Finding just the right program for these specific tastes among the thousands that are available isn't an easy task.

The makers of the Android Market were aware of this and took care to put in place a voting system that enables users to rate the programs. It's a five-star system in which more stars appear by an application's name as more users vote that they like it. The system also enables users to leave personal comments about the programs, providing more information when choosing a program to install on your cellphone.

One reason an application might be called advanced is that it is new and unique. For example, text editors (or word processors) have been around since the early days of computers, so an Android-specific text editor would not be considered advanced, even though it may be a well-written and valuable program to have on your Android phone.

However, a program that combines the power of location awareness and a running database of bus routes with the current time and date would offer a new and unique application that, if done well (with a quality interface and good responsiveness), would qualify as an advanced app.

Not to begrudge good text-editor programmers, but if they would throw in some eBook downloading capability or perhaps a voice-to-text module, they'd take more steps toward the "new and unique" front. Our point is that "advanced" is an arbitrary and subjective designation, so the programs that we highlight in this chapter depend on our particular likes and dislikes.

Apps by Categories

With thousands of available applications already in existence in these early days of Android technology, choosing to compare the advanced apps from the not-so-advanced apps is a daunting task. Just as everyone has unique needs, we selected advanced apps for this book based solely on what impressed us. Your proverbial mileage may vary.

Before continuing with our choices for advanced applications, a word of warning is due. The Android base software changes often: In only a few months, we've seen the SDK change from 1.0 to 1.1 to 1.5-pre to 1.5, using names like "cupcake" to designate the newest version of the base software. Quite possibly, such changes (sometimes made to your cellphone OTA—that is, over the air)—can break the functionality of a favorite advanced application. This is an unfortunate but, thankfully, rare event. Most of the time, the makers of the advanced applications are aware of these changes, and occasionally you'll be automatically informed of an updated version of the application that's available for download. We recommend that you always download these updated versions.

Having written all that, we now proceed to list advanced applications, divided by category and listed in alphabetical order.

Business Apps

Smart phones are rapidly replacing laptop computers as the businessperson's preferred portable computer. And why not? After all, the form factor is perfect.

Carrying a device in your pocket is a lot easier than lugging it in a suitcase of some kind. The raw computing power and storage capabilities of cellphones has increased to the point at which they actually can replace much of the business functionality on laptop computers. To some businesspeople, a smart phone is a portable computer first and a phone second!

Also, thanks to the connectivity to the Internet, as noted earlier, businesspeople can rely on a lot of computer power at the corporate office, as long as the cellphone can display that data in a useful way. As of this writing, Android has no business-compatible spreadsheet, word processing, database, or slideshow-presentation software, as some of the earlier, established cellphones do (such as those offered by Palm Computing), but this lack will be remedied in time. However, some generically useful programs are available in the Android Market, including some dedicated business calculators and useful programs for keeping tabs on your stock portfolio.

Having said all that, we begin with what we consider the current killer app of the Android cellphone, the Android Market, but there are additional applications like "Finance" and "Quote Pro" that you may find just as valuable:

- **Android Market**—This is the killer app of the cellphone business. It makes the search for useful software and utilities as easy as you can imagine. The designers of the Android Market created a system that enables users of Android cellphones to find software, examine its public rating, and read brief comments about the software before choosing to download it—and all this happens right on the cellphone. With just one click of the Market icon, the search begins. This is a powerful and easy-to-use advanced application that belies the complexity on the other end of the line.

- **Finance**—Written by Google insiders, Finance is an advanced application that currently supports only the U.S. stock exchanges. As we alluded to earlier, the real power of this program lies in its automatic synchronization with your personal portfolios stored in your Google Finance account. It provides you a lot of optional settings and views as well.

- **Quote Pro**—Similar to Finance, Quote Pro is a simple but powerful program for getting a quick, updated look at how your stock portfolio is doing. You enter the stock symbols that you want to track into Quote Pro's colorful display; the stock information then is updated every minute or so. (You can programmatically set the update rate, but we recommend sticking with the default rate.)

13

You can get more detailed information about any of the stocks or indexes by clicking the stock's symbol. Some of the best additional details are listings of news stories about any stock that you click. When you click one of these news stories, the built-in browser automatically executes with the URL of the news story passed to it. Priceless!

Communication Apps

The whole point of a cellphone is to enhance communications, so it comes as no surprise that this is one area where Android has well-established, highly useful applications already available. The Google suite of tools are highly integrated and easy to use, and provide useful information whenever it becomes available through the novel and well-designed Android notification system.

- **Gmail**—What can we say about Gmail other than that it will likely become your favorite Android cellphone application? The "right now" nature of email constantly commands your attention (for better or worse), and with its tight integration with the Android notification panel, Gmail is a perfect balance of form and function. As with most advanced applications that run on Android, what you see on the screen is the culmination of a lot of hard work that the Gmail servers have done in the background.

  Email is a highly abused medium, and the job of filtering spam isn't an easy task. Google's algorithms for this filtering task are highly sophisticated, and the pleasing result is not having to wade through so many unimportant emails every time you interact with the system. When it comes to software design, Google leaves the hard work to the Internet servers.

- **Webkit Browser**—When most people think of the Internet, it's usually in the form of the World Wide Web on a web browser. The web browser built into Android is the Webkit Browser. This powerful application is ideally suited—and was designed for—small display devices. The code base for the Webkit Browser is essentially Apple Computing's Safari browser. (You can read more about this particular advanced application in Chapter 12, "Developing Mobile Web Applications.")

Location-Based Apps

This new category of software came into existence because of the unique nature of cellphones: They are portable and can be made to know where they are at any moment. The HTC/T-Mobile G1 particularly excels at this; it can determine its approximate location using just the coordinates of the cell tower that it is currently locked to, but it also has a genuine GPS satellite receiver built into it. Getting a fix via the GPS takes a little longer than with the tower method, but this method has far better accuracy. Consider the advanced applications in this category:

- **GPS Status**—This app, from EclipSim, gives you detailed location and orientation information on a single display that is both visually pleasing and comprehensive. With information such as heading, orientation, pitch, latitude, longitude, accuracy, altitude, time of last fix, magnetic field flux, relative speed, acceleration in G force units, and a running count of the satellites that it is in contact with, you couldn't ask for a better program if you want to know where you are.

  Optionally, GPS Status enables you to choose the units to display the information in (distance in meters or feet, speed in kilometers per hour, miles per hour, meters per second, or knots; position in DD.DDDDDD, DD MM.MMM, or DD MM SS.S; and so on) and even provides a choice of color theme (default, daylight, or night).

  The default theme simulates the look of a pocket compass, with eye-catching yellow lines, red and blue pointers, and white text on a black background. This advanced application belongs on every Android cellphone, with a built-in GPS, accelerometer, and magnetic compass.

- **Maps**—The built-in Google Maps application has been around for a few years and can be run by many non-Android cellphones. It is an astounding application that, based on your current location, can display a list of nearby businesses, including restaurants, service stations, government buildings, and more. It can give you driving directions to any of these and can even be embedded into other applications to supplement their functionality. As a perfect example of this, the Weather Channel application (described later) can overlay Google Maps with weather information. Simply amazing!

  But there's more to Google Maps than being location based. You can enter any existing address, city, state, zip code, and more, and it will display that location and allow you to search for what is also nearby.

13

A TRUE STORY FROM ONE OF THE BOOK'S AUTHORS, BILL ZIMMERLY:

I was driving home from work one day, when I suddenly blew out a tire on the highway. Fortunately, I was able to safely make it off the highway, and I pulled into a nearby McDonald's parking lot. When the vehicle was safely parked, I pulled out my cellphone and fired up the Google Maps application. It took about 30 seconds for it to get a GPS fix on my exact location, and I entered a search for a nearby business using the keyword 'tires.' About 10 seconds after that, I knew that I was only about 400 feet from a Dobb's Tire and Auto shop on the other side of the McDonald's—but it had been hidden from view by intervening buildings. Knowing this, I started up my van and drove slowly and carefully right to the Dobb's Tire and Auto shop and had the blown tire replaced in less than an hour. If that doesn't define a useful location-based application, I don't know what does.

- **Sky Map**—For stargazers among us, this program is a real gem. It obtains a fix on your location using GPS and then, using the built-in magnetic compass of the T-Mobile G1, it displays a sky map of the area that you are directly looking at, as long as you're also staring at the G1 screen. This advanced application combines several of the built-in device's capabilities, giving that distinctive "wow factor" that geeks like us love to show off to other geeks.

  The default display shows constellation names in blue text on a black background, with pinkish lines connecting the stars to make the constellation look more like what it is supposed to be (a bear, an archer, a dog, a scorpion, and so on).

  It also displays and labels Messier objects from the Messier catalog using their assigned numbers. You can optionally have it display star names, constellation names, Messier object names, planets, the right ascension/declination grid, and the horizon. And as a great finishing touch, it can be set to automatically check for updates every time the program starts.

- **The Weather Channel**—As hinted at in the discussion on Google Maps, this advanced application is a powerful tool that can get a fix on your location and display a map with various weather information overlaid on it. It also enables you to specify a list of favorite locations so that you can check the local conditions on demand.

The main display is a brief summary of the conditions at all your favorite locations. By clicking any one of these, you can drill down to see greater detail about that location. It displays any local warnings with a button labeled View Alert. These can include tornado watches, severe thunderstorm warnings, or local flood warnings.

The specific-location page provides tabs for current conditions (date, current temperature, cloud condition, a "feels like" temperature, speed and direction vectored wind data, humidity, UV index, and visibility), an hourly display (of time, condition, temperature, precipitation, and wind vector averages), a 36-hour summary (today, tonight, tomorrow), and a 10-day forecast feature (date, condition, forecast, high/low temperatures, and precipitation expected).

This is a useful application for traveling and keeping tabs on the conditions that you're likely to see as you move through different cities and counties en route to your destination.

Entertainment Apps

This category depends the most on the user's individual taste. Many users prefer action-based "shoot 'em up" games, whereas others (like me!) prefer more traditional and cerebral games, such as chess. The entertainment category also encompasses more than just games; other advanced programs can appeal as well, such as the built-in MP3 player.

- **Abduction**—With impressive graphics, this is an addictive game involving cute little cows jumping from platform to platform until aliens can rescue them. It may sound corny, and it is, but it is a great time-waster when you have the time to waste. Abduction makes good use of the built-in accelerometer, sensing your tilt of the device in order to adjust the jumps. Beware of one thing—this game is so addictive that you may have difficulty getting back to work after a relaxing coffee break spent playing it.

- **Bonsai Blast**—By Glu Mobile, this game has great sound effects and the graphics are as impressive as the Abduction game. It is a puzzle game with plenty of bonuses and power-ups to keep you busy while time passes at the Dentist's office. The objective of the game is to clear out all of the colored balls before they reach the "yin yang" at the end of the level.

13

■ **Chess for Android**—This free program by Aart Bik plays a very enter-
taining game of the classic Persian game of chess. You don't even have
to play chess to have a good time with it: You can set it to play itself
while you watch the successive moves. Powerful, fast, and with good-
looking graphics, this is an impressive advanced application.

■ **Doom for Android**—This is a port of the wonderful old PC shoot 'em
up game that was popular in the 90s. The G1 has more than enough
computer power to make the scrolling smooth and keep the game
interesting. You have the option to load several different game plans
(called "WADs") as well as options that include playing the game in a
full screen mode and hearing action/adventure sounds while you play.
As with all of the games listed here, Doom for Android, which is free,
can be downloaded from the Android Market.

■ **MP3 player**—What is a good cellphone without the built-in capability
to play your favorite 'toons? The T-Mobile G1 and its Android music
player give you a quality MP3 player. You can even keep entire album
collections in your cellphone using large-capacity SD cards (8GB and
above) to hold MP3 files.

You also can store and play many more audio files. Podcasts, audio
books, Bibles (such as those narrated by Sir Alexander Scourby), university lectures, church sermons, and more are available for download
from numerous websites.

If you're an audiophile, the built-in Android MP3 player might quickly
become your favorite advanced application.

Utility Apps

Perhaps the most important program in this category is a backup utility for
saving important data in case the unthinkable happens. Unfortunately, no
"total backup" solution currently exists for Android. But it is only a matter of
time until one emerges—and when it does, get it!

■ **Astro File Manager**—Most of us who work with desktop or laptop
computers like to work on the files with an advanced file-browsing program. Microsoft Windows has the Windows File Explorer. Linux has
several such programs; many users like Nautilus. Under Android, the
Astro File Manager is a premier file manager that does much of what
its larger machine's cousins do. You can browse up, down, and around
the file system of both Android's internal flash memory and the
SD card. You can browse files based on their file extension, and you

can send files using Gmail or Messaging. You can also execute file operations such as edit, move, copy, and delete, as long as you have the proper access rights.

A killer app buried within the Astro File Manager, known as the Application Backup, enables you to automatically save backup copies of the executable files associated with all the applications in your Android cellphone. This program is worth it for that capability alone.

- **Power Manager**—One of the common complaints against the T-Mobile G1 was its small battery. It can run out of power quickly—too quickly. Although larger-capacity batteries are available, a partial solution for the power drain problem is this program for managing the resources of the device. You can specify various configurations based on its profiles for how you want the cellphone to use battery power. You specify how the devices are powered up (or not), to fine-tune the phone's power consumption. The default profiles are fine for most of us, in our opinion.

- **Terminal**—No self-respecting Linux-loving geek would be caught without a Linux command shell nearby. After all, it's therapeutic to "drop into the shell" and issue a few cd, ls, and cat commands once in a while—especially to impress your geek friends who have not as yet climbed onto the Android bandwagon.

Creating Advanced Apps

All applications begin with an idea. A single human being might experience a moment of need (such as wanting to know when the 43rd Street Bus will arrive) and then realize that the information is not only accessible on the Internet, but should be highly useful to other Android cellphone-carrying people on the go.

Of course, if the schedule is posted on the Internet, an Android cellphone user can access it by browsing the web page where the data is posted. But the Android cellphone is a time- and location-aware device. Why should the user be burdened with anything more than just clicking a Next Bus application icon and leaving the heavy lifting to the network? After all, it can't be difficult for the Next Bus application to pass the user's GPS coordinates to the network, and for the network to use those coordinates, the current time, and the bus-routing database to calculate and display the next bus, when it will arrive at the bus stop near the user, and how long the wait is expected to be.

Knowing all this *at a glance* means the user can instantly see if he has time enough to grab a cup of coffee before catching the bus, rather than spending that same time browsing the bus company's website for the schedule. This is how new advanced applications are conceived.

The next step in the process of creating an advanced Android application is to get it down on paper. Ideas can be fleeting: You must capture them and write them down before you forget them. (Of course, there are alternatives to writing on paper—other great ideas are typing the idea into a note on your Android cellphone or making an audio recording of the idea. The important thing is to record the idea before you forget it.)

After this, much depends on who and what you are. If you are a skilled Android programmer with time on your hands and you want to convert this idea to reality, then by all means, make it happen! Don't forget to use the Android community on Google Groups (http://groups.google.com). Be sure to search for groups that mention Android. If you get stuck or are having another problem, the community is there to help. Programming is easier when it is a community activity, and sharing knowledge is essential to building such a community. But if you don't have the time or you're a nonprogrammer with a good idea, contact a programmer. Just get on one of the Android discussion forums in Google Groups and ask for a programmer's help.

Programming Android isn't that difficult if you are already a computer programmer. Android is a Linux system with a Java-based high-level programming interface. The Android software development kit (SDK) is freely available for download, as is the most commonly used integrated development environment (IDE), known as Eclipse. Downloading and installing these tools is an easy task, and the only significant barrier remaining to creating an advanced application is practice and the skills required to do so.

13

APPENDIX

Troubleshooting

Electronics attract gremlins that make funny things happen in devices at unexpected times. What follows are a few of the issues that we've encountered while using and programming for the phone since its release in October 2008. This is by no means a complete list of the issues you might face with your Android-enabled device—every device is different. But these do appear to be common issues; hopefully, our answers will help you fix the problems that you face.

Your best option if you encounter a problem that we don't address here is to contact the wireless carrier or the device manufacturer for help. Some issues are covered under warranty. Be aware, though, that some are not, and the time you spend on the phone with tech support could be charged to you. You also might find that fixing the problem is expensive or time consuming.

Of course, we hope that's not something you have to face. Hopefully, you can solve any issues that you encounter using the suggestions offered in this appendix.

IN THIS APPENDIX

- ■ Troubleshooting Device Issues
- ■ Troubleshooting Application Issues
- ■ Troubleshooting Design Issues

Troubleshooting Device Issues

My phone doesn't ring for cellphone calls, but it does ring for landline calls. What did I do wrong?

You might not have done anything wrong. It could be a problem with the phone or just a bug. One way to see if it's a bug is to power off the phone and remove the battery. Allow the phone to sit without the battery for about 30 seconds, and then put the battery back in place and reboot the phone.

After the boot sequence, have different people call you from landline and cellphones to see if the problem has corrected itself. If not, take your phone to the dealer from which you purchased the phone.

My device doesn't see my wireless network. What can I do?

Check to ensure that your phone's wireless radio is enabled. Wireless should be enabled straight out of the box, but if you've changed any settings, you might have turned it off. To ensure that your wireless radio is on, from the Home screen, touch the **Menu** button and select **Settings.** Select **Wireless Controls** and ensure that the **Wi-Fi** option is selected. That enables the wireless capabilities, and you should now be able to detect your wireless network.

If enabling the phone's wireless capabilities is not the problem, you could have a hardware issue with your wireless capabilities. Take your phone to the dealer where you purchased it. There may also be a problem with the wireless network to which you are trying to connect. Ensure that the network is up and running and that you have permission to access it. If you're still having issues, contact the network administrator.

My screen froze and won't advance. What's wrong?

A screen freeze is usually caused by a conflict or application crash. Try powering off the device and then powering it back on. That should fix the problem.

If the phone is locked up and won't power off, remove the battery from the back of the device. Then reinsert it and reboot the phone. The screen should then work normally.

A

I changed the ringtones for my calls, and now my message notifications don't work. How do I reset them?

Message notifications are tied to the ringtone that you have set on the phone. Unless you set them separately, the notifications that you receive for email messages will be the same as the notifications that you receive for appointments and calls on your phone.

To set ringtones in each application, open the application and go to the settings screen. There you should see a ringtone option that enables you to change the ringtone for that specific application.

My screen is too bright. How do I fix it?

If your screen is too bright (or too dull), it's probably just a settings issue. Press the **Menu** key and then select **Settings**. On the settings screen, touch **Sound & Display** and then scroll to the bottom of the screen. Touch **Brightness** and then use the slider to adjust the brightness of the screen until you're satisfied.

There's no way to adjust the brightness of the backlighting on the keyboard, though.

I pressed the camera button, but the camera won't start. How do I fix it?

The camera won't start with a single button press. As part of a precaution to keep the camera from being accidentally activated, you must press and hold the camera button to activate the camera. Alternatively, you can put a link to the camera icon on your Home screen so you don't have to use the button.

My screen has black/white spots. How do I get rid of them?

Black or white spots on your screen are a good indication that there are dead pixels on the screen. Sometimes when pixels seem dead, they're actually just stuck. Try running a video onscreen that has quick color changes over a 2- or 3-minute span. If the pixel is simply stuck, this *might* unstick it.

More likely, the pixel truly is dead. If that's the case, either you have to live with these dead pixels or you can try getting a replacement device from the carrier that sold it to you. Fortunately, not many instances of dead pixels have been reported on the T-Mobile G1.

A

I need to take the battery out of my phone, but I can't figure out how to get the back off. Can you help?

The back of the G1 is fitted tightly to the rest of the device housing. However, it just snaps off. To take the back off the phone, open the keyboard and grasp the latch for the back of the device. Gently lift back, away from the phone body, until the back pops off.

It definitely feels like you're going to break the back of the phone, but this is how the battery cover is meant to be removed. As long as you're moving gently and not snapping off the cover, you should be able to remove it with no issues.

My calls aren't ringing through, and I don't get a missed call message. What's wrong?

It's probably a network issue. You can take the phone to the dealer from which you purchased it, but it's less time consuming to call the wireless carrier first and ask if they're experiencing problems with the network.

How do I update my device firmware?

If you're using a phone that's on the original wireless carrier's network, any firmware updates released are automatically delivered to your phone. The updates download automatically during a low traffic time; when the update has finished, you'll receive notification that it has been installed. You'll probably have to reboot the device to complete the update.

If you're using a device that has been unlocked for another wireless carrier, you might not receive over-the-air updates. Some over-the-air updates are placed on the Web, and you'll need to download and install them on your phone manually. However, not all updates are placed on the Web. This is one of the reasons why we don't recommend unlocking the phone for other networks.

The battery gets hot while the phone is charging. Is there a way to cool it down?

It's not uncommon for the battery to get warm while the phone is charging. However, if the phone gets hot to the touch or too hot to handle, unplug it immediately and take it to your nearest wireless dealer.

I don't get even a full day's use out of my phone. Is something wrong with my battery?

The batteries for the T-Mobile G1 are notoriously short in life. If you're using the phone to talk, message, and use wireless and GPS radios on, you might not get a full day's use out of the phone. You can extend the life of your battery by turning off all nonessential processes (such as wireless or GPS) when they're not in use. You might want to consider larger-capacity batteries, too—talk to your dealer or search the Internet for "G1 extended battery."

Cellphone batteries also tend to lose energy life over time. If you've had your phone for a while, that could be the problem. Replacing the battery with a new *OEM (original equipment manufacturer)* should provide better battery life. Make sure the battery you choose is original equipment, however, as knock-offs (while cheaper) could damage your phone.

I can access the Android Market when I connect via my wireless network, but not when I try using 3G.

Some carriers require you to prove that you are authorized before they allow you to make your first connection. This is usually a simple process they can fix for you when you call them.

Troubleshooting Application Issues

I can't place icons on the right or left side of my Home page. What's wrong?

Placing an icon on either the right or left side of the Home page requires some patience. First long-press the icon until you feel it vibrate; then, without breaking the touch, drag the icon to the right or left side of the screen. When you reach the right or left boundary, hold the icon there for 2 or 3 seconds, and the screen should scroll over.

Just drop the icon wherever you want it on the screen. You might need a couple tries to get this motion down; it's easy to get to the edge of the screen and move a bit too far. The result is dropping the icon at the edge of the screen.

I accidentally deleted an icon that I want to have on my desktop. How do I get it back?

To place an icon on your desktop (including replacing one you deleted but want back), open the applications menu. Then long-touch the icon that you want to place on the desktop. When the device vibrates, the apps menu disappears and you can drop the icon at the spot on the Home page where you want it to reside.

A

Every time I try to start an application, I get a force-close message. Now what?

Some applications, especially third-party apps, crash upon loading. If you encounter an application that force-closes every time you try to open it, try removing the application (refer back to Chapter 9, "Adding Applications to Your Device," for instructions on how to do that). You can then try to reinstall it, to see if that fixes the problem. Sometimes, however, it's best to wait a few days before you try to reinstall an application that you've removed for technical issues. Usually the developer will reprogram the app to fix the problem.

Everything is moving slow on my phone. What do I do?

The applications could be trying to do too much at one time. Try powering off the phone and then rebooting it. If this doesn't fix the problem, you might have too many applications installed; consider removing some.

One of my applications is draining my battery life. How do I fix it?

Some applications tap into other resources, such as your GPS system or your wireless network. If you have an application that seems to be draining the life out of your battery, check the application settings to make sure your phone isn't activating the wireless or the GPS each time it reboots or the application starts. You might also want to consider buying a larger-capacity battery: Ask your dealer or search the Internet for "G1 extended battery."

How do I reset my phone to factory settings on a T-Mobile G1?

You can reset your G1 phone. The first way is to perform a factory data reset. Starting from the Home screen, press the **Menu** key and then select **Settings**. Touch **SD Card & Phone Storage** and then touch **Factory Data Reset**. You'll receive a confirmation prompt. If you're certain that you want to reset the phone, then touch the **Reset Phone** button. Just be aware that after you perform this reset, you'll lose all your stored data and the downloaded applications that you've put on your phone.

The other way to reset the phone is to perform a hard reset. However, you should perform a hard reset only if the device can't be reset through the previous option. If you have no choice but to use a hard reset on your phone, you can follow these steps:

1. Power off the device completely.

2. Press and hold the **Home** and **Power** buttons for 20–25 seconds. The device cycles through the home screen and then a black screen with a **Warning** sign appears.

3. Slide open the keyboard and press the **Alt+W** keys.

4. Press the **Home** and **Back** keys. The phone should now reboot. When the reboot is complete, the device should be restored to factory settings. If the device won't restart when you press the **Home** and **Back** keys, take the battery out of the device, replace it, and reboot the device with the power button.

Remember, when you reset the device to factory settings, you'll lose all the contacts, files, pictures, and any other data you have stored on the phone. I recommend that you back up the information before you perform the reset.

Troubleshooting Design Issues

I wrote an application in the emulator that connects to the Internet, but when I run it on a G1, it just hangs with no error message.

This is probably because your application hasn't set the correct permission to connect to the Internet in its `AndroidManifest.xml`. By default, apps running in the emulator can access the Internet without it. Physical handsets cannot because this is a permission the user must grant upon installation—it could cost them money. Add this line in the <manifest> section of `AndroidManifest.xml`:

```
<uses-permission android:name="android.permission.INTERNET">
➥</uses-permission>
```

My app doesn't seem to connect to certain Internet addresses.

This could be for many reasons. The carrier might be censoring some addresses based on their name, country, or even MIME content. Try connecting via Wi-Fi instead of the carrier (3G). If this now works, it is because your ISP is allowing traffic that your carrier was not.

Another tip is to try to connect using Android's web browser instead of your app. If you can enter the URL in the address bar and it, too, cannot connect, you can be sure it is not your app, but some other connection issue.

A

How do I emulate the trackball ? The onscreen buttons send only left, right, up, down, and center events.

Press and hold the Del key while moving your mouse. You'll see a little graphical representation of the trackball you can then move accordingly.

I see many examples of full projects, for example, in the Google code repositories, which have the same folder structure. How can I quickly get these into Eclipse as a workable project?

In Eclipse, choose New, Android Project and then set Contents to Create Project from Existing Source. Android projects use a standard folder layout to make this sort of operation easier.

How can I add a third-party JAR file to my project that isn't part of the standard Android development system?

Create a folder from the root of your project called, for example, lib. Place the JAR file there. Then use Project, Properties, Java Build Path, Libraries, Add JARs and select it.

I've written a game that involves animation on the screen, but it's jerky. What can I do to improve things?

The first thing this sounds like is that Android's garbage collector is interrupting your code when you don't want it to, and the time it takes to do its work is causing this effect. To verify this, in the emulator, turn on full debugging and observe the LogCat view in the DDMS window. Every time a garbage collection occurs, you will see an entry for it, and these will coincide with your onscreen glitches.

The solution is to stop causing so many garbage collections. Understanding that they occur when objects are created and destroyed is essential to this. If you have a loop in your code, study carefully every place "new" is used, either directly or indirectly via a method call, and consider preallocating these instances as member variables in your class (where possible). This is a tradeoff between memory usage and performance, and is a large subject to cover sufficiently.

Continue observing the garbage collection frequency in the DDMS windows each time you tune your code, to avoid them. Hopefully you will see less of them and your animation will run more smoothly.

A

My app sometimes needs time to process an operation. How can I get rid of the "Force Close or Wait" message that the G1 shows after 5 seconds?

You can't. This is a hardwired safety feature built into Android to prevent the whole handset from locking up. However, things aren't as bad as they seem. The handset does this only if it notices that the UI on your app has stopped responding. So you can change your app to conduct the processing in a separate thread, while keeping the main UI responsive.

It's cumbersome starting the emulator for each run. Can I speed this up?

Yes, you don't need to restart it each time. Just leave it running in its own window. When you run your app from Eclipse, you'll see it stop running on the emulator and start fresh again.

There have been several SDK releases. Do I need to worry about which device firmware my builds target?

Generally, the carriers do a great job of updating users' handsets over the air, so you can be confident that they will be running the latest stable versions. The Android SDK version will always be compatible with this. In the traditional handset business, this was a huge problem; users were advised to take their handsets to their dealers for an upgrade or to buy a new model, neither of which really happened in practice. Android prompts users when new updates are available and they tend to accept them, so you're pretty safe nowadays.

The other concern is if your app uses features that become obsolete in future Android versions. This happened occasionally during the SDK's early days, before any handsets were launched. In such a case, the workarounds are always fully documented by Google. You need to implement these and rerelease your app, so check out their Android development sites for more information.

I read that you cannot deploy your app unless it has been signed. When I connect my G1 via USB and run it, I see it on the handset just fine. How is this so?

Your app has been signed behind the scenes with a special development certificate created just for this purpose. This is just to get you up and running with the minimum of fuss; you will find you cannot distribute any apps to other handsets that you create this way.

A

G1 Keyboard Shortcuts

Using a tiny QWERTY keyboard isn't the easiest thing to do. Neither is navigating commands on a touch-screen device. Fortunately, shortcuts make it easier for you to accomplish tasks.

These shortcuts fall into three different categories: text and typing, application navigation, and browser shortcuts. Some of them you'll use all the time. Others are slightly obscure but come in handy now and then, so keep the list nearby as a reference.

Notice that the special characters used in these listings are the actual appearance of the key on the keyboard. Where you see arrows or magnifying glasses, look for those keys to use in keyboard combinations.

B

Shortcuts for Navigating Text and Typing

Insert Special Character	Alt+spacebar
Delete Character	Del (for character to the left)
	↑+DEL (for character to the right)
Delete Line	Alt+Del
Caps Lock	Press ↑ twice
Jump to Beginning or End of a Line	Alt+trackball (left or right)
Tab	Alt+Q
Highlight Text	↑+trackball (left or right)
Cut Text	Menu+X, or long-touch highlighted text to open menu and select **Cut**
Copy Text	Menu+C, or long-touch highlighted text to open menu and select **Copy**
Paste Text	Menu+V, or long-touch highlighted text to open menu and select **Paste**
Undo	Menu+Z
Select All	Menu+A
Insert Symbol	Press Alt twice, press Alt+spacebar, or long-touch letters with special characters (A, E, I, O, U, N, and S)

Shortcuts for Navigating Applications

Open Contacts	🔍 +C
Open Email (not Gmail)	🔍 +E
Open Gmail	🔍 +G
Open Calendar	🔍 +L
Open Instant Messaging	🔍 +I
Open Maps	🔍 +M
Open Music	🔍 +P
Open YouTube	🔍 +Y
Directions in Maps	Menu+D
Map Mode	Menu+M
Map History	Menu+H
My Location (in Maps)	Menu+0 (zero)
Map Settings	Menu+P
Zoom in to Map	Menu+I
Zoom out of Map	Menu+O (letter O)

Forward Message (in Gmail)	F
Reply to Message (in Gmail)	R
Reply to All (in Gmail)	A
Archive Message	Y

Browser Shortcuts

Open Browser	SEARCH+B
Page Down	Spacebar
Page Up	↑+spacebar
Jump to the End of a List	Alt+trackball (roll down)
Jump to the Beginning of a List	Alt+trackball (roll up)
Open Browser Search	Menu+S
Open Bookmarks	Menu+B
Open Window	Menu+W
View History	Menu+H
Refresh Page	Menu+R
Back Up One Page	Menu+J
Forward One Page	Menu+K
Go to Home Page	Menu+spacebar
Zoom In	Menu+I
Zoom Out	Menu+O (letter O)
Open Address Bar	Menu+L
Open a Link in a New Window	Menu+click the link

Index

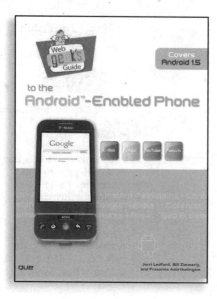

FREE Online Edition

Your purchase of **Web Geek's Guide to the Android Enabled Phone** includes access to a free online edition for 45 days through the Safari Books Online subscription service. Nearly every Que book is available online through Safari Books Online, along with more than 5,000 other technical books and videos from publishers such as Addison-Wesley Professional, Cisco Press, Exam Cram, IBM Press, O'Reilly, Prentice Hall, and Sams.

SAFARI BOOKS ONLINE allows you to search for a specific answer, cut and paste code, download chapters, and stay current with emerging technologies.

Activate your FREE Online Edition at www.informit.com/safarifree

> **STEP 1:** Enter the coupon code: XKDGNCB.

> **STEP 2:** New Safari users, complete the brief registration form.
> Safari subscribers, just log in.

If you have difficulty registering on Safari or accessing the online edition, please e-mail customer-service@safaribooksonline.com